JUSTICE TALKING

CENSORING
THE WEB

from NPR

★ ★ ★

LEADING ADVOCATES DEBATE
TODAY'S MOST CONTROVERSIAL ISSUES

CENSORING
THE WEB

Written and edited by
Kathryn Kolbert with Zak Mettger

THE NEW PRESS | New York

The publisher is grateful for permission to reprint the following copyrighted material:
"Digital Chaperones for Kids." Copyright © 2001 by Consumers Union of
U.S., Inc., Yonkers, New York, a nonprofit organization.
Reprinted with permission from the March 2001 issue of *Consumer Reports*,
for educational purposes only. No commercial use or photocopying permitted.
To learn more about Consumers Union, log onto www.ConsumerReports.org.

"First Amendment Timeline" reprinted with permission of www.freedomforum.org.

Published in the United States by The New Press, New York, 2001
Distributed by W. W. Norton & Company, Inc., New York

LIBRARY OF CONGRESS CATALOGING-IN-PUBLICATION DATA
Justice talking : leading advocates debate today's most controversial issues—
censoring the web / [written and edited by] Kathryn Kolbert with Zak Mettger.
        p.   cm.—(Justice talking audio book series)
            Includes bibliographical references.
            ISBN 1-56584-715-6 (pbk. & CD)
1. Censorship—United States.   2. Internet—Law and legislation—United States.
            3. Pornography—Law and legislation—United States.
        4. Freedom of speech—United States.   5. Internet and children.
        I. Kolbert, Kathryn.   II. Mettger, Zak.   III. Series.
                        KF4775 .J87 2001
                343.7309'944—dc21   2001030977

The New Press was established in 1990 as a not-for-profit alternative to the large, commercial publishing houses currently dominating the book publishing industry. The New Press operates in the public interest rather than for private gain, and is committed to publishing, in innovative ways, works of educational, cultural, and community value that are often deemed insufficiently profitable.

The New Press
450 West 41st Street, 6th floor
New York, NY 10036
www.thenewpress.com

Printed in Canada

2 4 6 8 10 9 7 5 3 1

CONTENTS

SERIES PREFACE

Justice Talking: Bringing the Constitution to Life

The United States Constitution is an extraordinary document that has enabled this nation to achieve a level of individual liberty and representative democracy unparalleled in the world. As the country's preeminent rule of law, the Constitution not only spells out the structure of American democracy and the individual liberties in which we take so much pride, it provides a framework for courts and policy makers to balance the rights and responsibilities of individuals, government, and society.

Although most Americans believe that an informed citizenry is essential for the Constitution to work as intended, many Americans remain largely uninformed about the 213-year-old document and the workings of our courts. A poll conducted by the National Constitution Center reveals that more of our nation's youth could name the Three Stooges than could name the three branches of government. Ninety-four percent of those surveyed knew the name of the star of television's *Fresh Prince of Bel Air,* while fewer than 3 percent (2.2%) could name the Chief Justice of the United States Supreme Court. For the most part, our nation's media have not done enough to improve the public's knowledge or understanding of constitutional issues, too often portraying the complex and fractious policy debates as competing thirty-second sound bites. Nor have the schools adequately met the challenge of providing civics lessons that engage our youth. Too often the Constitution and civics are taught exclusively as "early American history" rather than as a set of principles that have currency and import in the modern age.

The Annenberg Public Policy Center at the University of Pennsylvania has created *Justice Talking* and this audio book series to remind Americans that the Constitution is alive and well and still guiding all three branches of government as they make the critical decisions that shape our democracy. Beyond providing engaging and informative debates, we hope that *Justice Talking* and this book-and-CD set provide a model for debating complex and fractious social policy issues. Although our advocates often strongly disagree with one another, we hope that their discussion is respectful and thoughtful. If, at the end of reading and listening to this audio book, you think about the issue differently or recognize the validity of opposing views, we've done our job.

Most important, we hope the *Justice Talking* series will bring the Constitution to life and demonstrate that constitutional principles are neither abstract nor static but are evolving principles that affect our everyday lives. As Supreme Court Justice William Brennan has noted:

> Current Justices read the Constitution in the only way that we can: as twentieth-century Americans. We look to the history of the time of framing and to the intervening history of interpretation. But the ultimate question must be: What do the words of the text mean in our time? For the genius of the Constitution rests not in any static meaning it may have had in a world that is dead and gone, but in the adaptability of its great principles to cope with current problems and current needs. Our Constitution was not intended to preserve a pre-existing society, but to make a new one.*

---

* William Brennan, speech at Georgetown University: "The Constitution of the United States: Contemporary Ratification" (Oct. 12, 1985), reprinted in A. Mason and D. Stephenson, *American Constitutional Law* 607 (1987).

The *Justice Talking* Series

Each book in this series—which will cover issues of Web censorship, school vouchers, affirmative action, gun control, the death penalty, symbolic speech, and other contemporary topics—examines how a particular issue has been interpreted by advocates, the courts, lawmakers, the media, and the public. Without taking sides, we present conflicting arguments, statistics, studies, and analyses that will help you better understand the issues, come to your own conclusions, and enable you to be a more informed and thoughtful participant in policy debates that affect you, your community, and the nation. Each book in the series comes with a compact disk of a debate between two of the nation's experts on the issue, originally aired as part of National Public Radio's (NPR) *Justice Talking*.

This book on Web censorship considers whether laws enacted by the federal government to prevent children from viewing pornography on the Internet go too far in limiting children's and adults' access to the World Wide Web. The constitutional question is whether these federal and state laws that target materials deemed "harmful to minors" violate the right to free speech. The book outlines the policy arguments on both sides of the debate. It also contains excerpts from several important legal decisions, and a list of organizations, Web sites, and other resources that you can contact to learn more. And on page 151 you'll find a glossary of legal terms used in the book, to help you with concepts and expressions drawn from what for many of us is a foreign language.

More About *Justice Talking*

NPR's *Justice Talking* is a radio program that explores the controversies that come before our nation's courts and challenge our nation's conscience. Hosted by NPR's Margot Adler, *Justice Talking* features prominent advocates from throughout the political spectrum debating "hot button" issues of constitutional law: school vouchers, Web censorship, hate speech, and more. Some of these thorny social policy issues, like the death penalty and gun control, have been sources of controversy for many years. Others, like Web censorship and school vouchers, are taken right out of today's headlines. Produced by the Annenberg Public Policy Center at the University of Pennsylvania, the show is distributed by NPR to public radio stations nationwide and to NPR Worldwide as well.

Justice Talking shows are taped before a live audience at Carpenters' Hall in Philadelphia, the home of the First Continental Congress and just steps from the Liberty Bell. As you'll find from listening to the enclosed compact disk and reading the verbatim transcripts, each show is based on an actual lawsuit. The program begins with a background report prepared by a public radio correspondent that provides the human story behind the legal controversy, followed by opening statements from the guests. Ms. Adler then questions the guests and fields questions from the audience. For a complete list of past and upcoming shows, and to find out if, when, and where *Justice Talking* airs in your community, check out the show's Web site at www.justicetalking.org.

About Margot Adler

Margot Adler is an award-winning National Public Radio correspondent who is chief of NPR's New York Bureau. During her thirty years on public radio, Adler has been a regular contributor to *All Things Considered*, *Morning Edition*, and *Weekend Edition* and regularly brings clarity, depth, and insight to contemporary public issues. Adler received her B.A. degree from the University of California at Berkeley and her M.A. degree from the Graduate School of Journalism at Columbia University. She was a Nieman Fellow at Harvard University in 1981.

More About the Organizations
That Support *Justice Talking*

The Annenberg Public Policy Center, which produces *Justice Talking*, was created in 1994 by publisher and philanthropist Walter Annenberg as a community of scholars within the University of Pennsylvania's Annenberg School for Communication. Directed by Kathleen Hall Jamieson, the Center supports research, the development of educational resources, and media, lectures, and conferences in four areas: the effect of technology and information on society; the impact of media on children, education, and public values; the media and contemporary political discourse; and public awareness of health policy (see www.appc.org).

Generous support for the radio program, this book-and-CD set, and a multistate educational program that has been developed from the radio shows comes from the Annenberg Foundation, the Pew Charitable Trusts, and the Deer Creek Foundation, as well as from the National Constitution Center (NCC), a sponsor of the show. Congress established the NCC in 1987 to increase public awareness and understanding of the Constitution, its history, and its relevance to our daily lives. In September 2000 the NCC began building the first-ever museum devoted to honoring and explaining the Constitution. Located on Independence Mall in Philadelphia, the interactive museum is expected to open in spring 2003 (see www.constitutioncenter.org).

A Personal Note from Kathryn Kolbert

In my many years of practicing law—primarily as an advocate for women's rights—I often saw that the controversies that come before our nation's courts spark not only strong disagreement among differing interest groups but deep reflection about the values we hold dear. Many times in our recent history, Supreme Court deliberations on such issues as the death penalty, Web censorship, affirmative action, and abortion have highlighted the deep divisions in our society and forced the High Court to be concerned with its own institutional integrity and capacity to establish law that will be followed and respected by all. I'm convinced now more than ever that the public's understanding and commitment to democracy and fundamental fairness deeply affects the Court's deliberations. And while early in my legal career I believed that a wise judiciary settled the nation's disputes, I now believe that a wise public leads the Court to sound and fair resolutions. I hope that after reading this book and listening to these intriguing *Justice Talking* debates, you will feel better able to participate in the public discourse, for our fundamental constitutional liberties are best preserved with your help and vigilance.

ACKNOWLEDGMENTS

Justice Talking and this audio book would be impossible without the support and creativity of many. Kathleen Hall Jamieson, dean of the Annenberg School for Communications and director of the Annenberg Public Policy Center at the University of Pennsylvania, had the initial idea for the project and has provided the Annenberg Public Policy Center as a home base for all of us fortunate to work on the program. *Justice Talking* would have been impossible without her vision and the support of both the policy center and the university. I am especially grateful.

Justice Talking is also fortunate to have the support of a loyal group of sponsors and funders including the Annenberg Foundation, the Pew Charitable Trusts, the Deer Creek Foundation, Findlaw.com, and the Educational Foundation of America. Their support has been invaluable.

The National Constitution Center (now being built on Independence Mall) is a new national museum dedicated to the Constitution and has specifically donated to this book series. I appreciate their support of *Justice Talking* and look forward to working with them in the future.

Particular thanks to Zak Mettger, who dropped everything to write this book and spent months learning the issues and making them understandable. And to the American Bar Association Division on Public Education, which is helping to create "A Listening and Learning Guide" for teachers that will accompany this book.

Margot Adler's willingness to devote innumerable hours to *Justice Talking* has been a blessing. Her intelligence and charm and nearly thirty years' experience on public radio has made her the show's principal asset, and we are appreciative. National Public Radio, our new partner in this venture, has lent its significant endorsement of *Justice Talking*. I thank them and look forward to working closely in the future to showcase the program on NPR member stations.

The creative genius of the *Justice Talking* staff cannot go by without recognition. They have worked tirelessly to create and market *Justice Talking* and our other related projects and are responsible for its success. Julie Drizin, Sheryl Flowers, Kara McGuirk, Gary Kalman, and Erin Mooney make my life considerably better. Many thanks. Thanks as well to all of our student interns—particularly Sara Berger and Morgen Cheshire, who worked on this book—set-up reporters, engineers at Clear Sound, and all of the brilliant lawyers and advocates and members of our audience who add their insight each week.

Thanks as well to the Carpenters' Company of the City and County of Philadelphia, which owns and operates Carpenters' Hall. This historic building, the home of the nation's First Continental Congress, is a wonderful setting to debate the meaning and protections of the Constitution.

Last, but most important, a special thanks to my family: Joann, Sam, and Kate for their good humor, love, and support. My life is all the richer for it, and I'm grateful.

JUSTICE TALKING

CENSORING
THE WEB

PART I

CLEANSPEAK:
A LOOK AT
WEB CENSORSHIP

★ ★ ★ ★ ★ ★ ★ ★ ★ ★ ★ ★ ★ ★ ★ ★ ★

Porn on the Web: Are Restrictions Permissible?

The Internet is a great way to talk with friends, do research, read movie and record reviews, and shop for absolutely anything. And it's just as popular with children as adults, if not more so. According to a recent survey, in 1998, sixteen million children under age eighteen were using the Internet, nearly double the number in 1997, and six million of those kids were twelve or younger.[1] Children use the Internet to send and receive e-mail, talk to each other in chat rooms, hold "real-time" conversations with instant messaging, and get information of all kinds from the World Wide Web.

Many people, especially parents, are concerned, however, that along with all this useful (or at least inoffensive) information, the Internet also contains a great deal of "adult" content, a thinly disguised code word for pornography. Current estimates put the number of sites that display and sell pornographic material at more than thirty thousand.[2]

Parents, libraries, schools, and governments are asking what can be done to limit children's access to potentially harmful hard-core pornographic sites on the Internet. Can limits be imposed that avoid major damage to the First Amendment, which guarantees all of us the right to say, read, and look at nearly anything we want to without government interference?

Traditional solutions that have been used to restrict other obscene materials may not be appropriate or effective. The Internet is not a physical entity like a book or magazine that can be banned or wrapped in plain brown paper. It doesn't occupy any specific physical space, like a bookstore or movie house that can be shut down or forced to move. And using it is almost always an individual activity, which is hard to monitor without raising privacy concerns. These unique features make it hard—some say impossible—for the government, parents, or anyone else to control or limit what children see on the Internet. As this chapter demonstrates, people have strong views on whether pornographic content on the Internet should be restricted, how it can be done, and by whom.

Arguments for Government Restriction

- The prevalence of pornography in society leads to a decline in family values and respect for others. In particular, hard-core pornography dehumanizes women and children and may contribute to crime and abusive behavior directed against them.
- Children have easy access to pornography and sexually explicit chat rooms online. Parents cannot supervise their children's use of the Internet all the time, and current filtering and blocking software is not sophisticated enough to keep out *all* offensive material.
- Although distributing obscene materials to minors—by whatever means—is illegal, existing federal and state laws governing obscenity do not adequately protect young Internet users.
- Pedophiles have easy access to children online through chat rooms and instant messaging. The easy availability of pornography that attracts minors gives pedophiles even greater access.
- The easy availability of pornography on the Internet discourages many parents from paying for online access, for fear that their children will be exposed to pornography.
- Filtering software can be programmed to avoid infringing upon adults' First Amendment rights.

If we lose our kids to cyberporn, free speech won't matter.[3]
Christian Nelson, Rockford, Illinois

Arguments Against Government Restriction

- Permitting censorship on the Internet will open the door to increased private and public censorship throughout society.
- There is no effective way to determine whether an Internet user is an adult or a child, so any limits imposed on children will affect adults, violating their constitutionally guaranteed right to free speech.
- Decisions about what children should and should not look at on the Internet must be left to parents, who are best able to determine which materials are appropriate for their children.
- Existing federal and state laws governing obscenity are sufficient to protect children from pornography on the Internet.
- Any single definition of "obscene" or "harmful to minors" is highly subjective and varies from culture to culture, and community to community, over time. The government should not have the authority to define these terms and impose its views on everyone.
- Current filtering or blocking software and proposals are far too broad. They would screen out a good deal of nonpornographic material that is useful to children and adults alike.
- Little if any accurate data demonstrates that pornography causes or contributes to the physical or sexual abuse of women or children.

The issue of computer pornography has been blown way out of proportion. . . . My friends and I have access to [pornography,] and we don't look at it. The U.S. government has no right to censor the Internet or computer bulletin boards.[4]
Sara Burns, 17, Moscow, Ohio

Congress shall make no law respecting an establishment of religion, or prohibiting the free exercise thereof; or abridging the freedom of speech, or of the press; or the right of the people peaceably to assemble, and to petition the government for a redress of grievances.

First Amendment to the U.S. Constitution

Freedom of Speech: A Fundamental Constitutional Right

The founding fathers who pushed for a Bill of Rights—the first ten amendments to the U.S. Constitution—wanted to make sure that the rights and liberties of individual Americans were protected from potential abuses by the new federal government.[5] Chief among the founders' concerns was to assure citizens of the right of free expression. This concern resulted in adoption of the First Amendment.

According to the Freedom Forum, a nonpartisan foundation that works to protect a free press and free speech:

> Free speech is, arguably, the right most essential to democratic government. Without free speech and its other First Amendment cousins—freedom of the press, of assembly and of petition (rights collectively referred to as "freedom of expression")—citizens couldn't say what they believe, couldn't debate the actions of government at home and abroad, and couldn't analyze the wisdom and weaknesses of their elected leaders. Free speech is vital to peaceful social change—and it's the first right to go when tyrants take over.[6]

In the United States, First Amendment guarantees apply to all kinds of written and spoken words, including books, newspapers, magazines, and broadcast media. Free speech protections also extend to speech combined with action, such as picketing and demonstrations, and to symbolic speech, which encompasses paintings, plays, musical compositions, clothing, flag waving, and even flag burning. The First Amendment even protects the freedom not to speak. The government cannot, for example, force you to take a loyalty oath or recite the Declaration of Independence.[7]

The U.S. Supreme Court has long held that in most circumstances,[8] free expression deserves the highest standard of constitutional protection. Thus, anytime the government wants to restrict speech, it must give a compelling reason for it and must then design the restriction carefully, to make sure it is "narrowly tailored"—that is, limiting *only* the particular speech that the government is concerned about, without spilling over onto other forms of speech.[9] Only when these two conditions are met will the Supreme Court allow the restrictions to stand. Thanks to this remarkable level of constitutional protection, Americans are free to say and write what they like and to gather in large numbers to demonstrate and picket, distribute leaflets, and otherwise protest things, including government actions of which they disapprove.

Yet freedom of speech does have limits, as Supreme Court decisions have established over the years. When speech moves to action, for example, the government can take steps to protect the public. Thus, while the police cannot arrest protesters for chanting or singing, they can arrest them for blocking public buildings. And an overriding government interest—such as preserving national security or ensuring a fair trial—can take precedence over free speech concerns. For example, soldiers do not have the right to give away military secrets, witnesses are not free to lie under oath, and commercial advertisers may not make fraudulent claims. The government also can limit the "time, place, and manner" of speech in order to ensure public safety. It can require demonstrators to obtain a parade permit, for example, or enact a noise ordinance to prevent an excessive public disturbance. But the government can impose these restrictions only if they are clear and uniformly applied, so that certain demonstrators are not singled out due to the content of their speech—due to what they say, as opposed to where and when they say it.[10]

The Supreme Court has determined as well that certain types of speech are not constitutionally protected. These types include "defamation," "fighting words," or words that incite "imminent lawless action."[11] Most relevant to this chapter, the Court has also found that "obscene speech" and speech that is "harmful to minors" fall outside First Amendment protection.[12] But as the next section shows, coming up with an acceptable legal definition of "obscenity," one that is neither too broad nor too narrow, has confounded the courts for more than one hundred years. A timeline of important First Amendment decisions can be found on page 117.

What Is Obscene?

Until 1957 courts used a test established in 1868 by the Lord Chief Justice of England to determine whether a particular work was obscene. The guideline instructed courts to consider "whether the tendency of the matter charged . . . is to deprave and corrupt those whose minds are open to such immoral influences and into whose hands a publication of this sort may fall."[13]

Responding to growing criticism that this test was outdated, in 1957 the U.S. Supreme Court adopted a new test in *Roth v. United States*, 354 U.S. 476 (1957), a case involving a man convicted of sending obscene books, photos, and advertisements through the mail. In this landmark decision, the Court found that materials would be considered obscene if "to the average person, applying contemporary community standards, the dominant theme of the material taken as a whole appeals to prurient interest."

Even with this new test, however, state and federal courts continued to struggle with what is or is not obscene. So, in 1973, in *Miller v. California*, 413 U.S. 15 (1973), the Supreme Court established a more detailed three-part test that governments should use to decide whether a picture, book, movie, or other material is "obscene":

- whether the average person, applying contemporary community standards,[14] would find that the work, taken as a whole, appeals to the prurient interest,
- whether the work depicts or describes, in a patently offensive way, sexual conduct . . . specifically defined by the applicable state laws, and
- whether the work, taken as a whole, lacks serious literary, artistic, political, or scientific value.[15]

[T]he only honest definition we've ever had of . . . obscenity from the Supreme Court is Potter Stewart's famous dictum . . . "I cannot define [pornography], but I know it when I see it."[16]
ACLU President Nadine Strossen, on *Justice Talking*

This three-part test remains the standard used today, except for cases involving the distribution of pornographic materials to children under age seventeen. In a 1968 case, *Ginsberg v. New York*, 390 U.S. 629 (1968), the Supreme Court created extra protections for these children because of the government's compelling interest in protecting their welfare. The Court held that governments can bar the distribution of material considered harmful to minors, even if it would not qualify as obscene when circulated to adults. Even so, the Court has made clear that governments must be extremely careful in applying the "harmful to minors" standard, in order to avoid vague, open-ended restrictions on free speech and reducing "the adult population . . . to reading only what is fit for children."[17]

The Federal Government—and the Courts—Get into the Act

The federal government's first attempt to protect children from pornography on the Internet came in 1996, when Congress passed the Communications Decency Act (CDA). One of the law's provisions made it a crime "knowingly" to transmit "obscene or indecent" messages to any person under eighteen years of age.[18] A second provision prohibited the "knowing" sending or displaying to a person under eighteen of any message "that, in context, depicts or describes, in terms patently offensive as measured by contemporary community standards, sexual or excretory activities or organs."[19] Penalties included up to two years in jail and/or a $250,000 fine.

> *The only barriers between children and pornographic pictures on the Internet are perfunctory onscreen warnings which inform minors that they are on their honor not to look. . . . [This is] like taking a porn shop and putting it in the bedroom of your children and then saying "Do not look."*[20]
>
> Senator Dan Coats (R-Ind.),
> cosponsor, Communications Decency Act of 1996

ACLU v. Reno I and *II*

On February 8, 1996, the same day President Bill Clinton signed the Communications Decency Act into law, the American Civil Liberties Union (ACLU) and a number of other organizations including Human Rights Watch, Electronic Privacy Information Center, Computer Professionals for Social Responsibility, and Planned Parenthood Federation of America sued Attorney General Janet Reno and the U.S. Department of Justice. The lawsuit argued that the CDA's "indecent transmission" and "patently offensive display" provisions were unconstitutional because they would impose criminal penalties for free expression protected by the First Amendment. The complaint also decried the law's definitions as vague and overbroad, noting, for example, that the words "indecent" and "patently offensive" were not explained with enough precision to give people fair warning of what they or their children could look at without breaking the law. The law's likely effect, according to the ACLU, would be to discourage people from using the Internet. This is what the courts call a "chilling effect" on free speech.

The three-judge District Court panel assembled to hear the case agreed that the two provisions aimed at protecting juveniles would stifle free speech by adults.[21] The panel rejected the federal government's arguments that the CDA contained adequate protections—credit card verification, adult access codes, and personal identification numbers—to ensure that adults' access to the Internet would not be curtailed. The government filed an appeal with the U.S. Supreme Court, which in June 1997 upheld the lower court's ruling by a vote of 7–2, agreeing with its conclusion that the CDA "places an unacceptably heavy burden on protected speech, and . . . threatens to torch a large segment of the Internet community." *ACLU v. Reno II*, 521 U.S. 844, 881 (1997).[22]

The government's arguments in favor of the CDA were unpersuasive, the Court said, including its contention that the restrictions were in keeping with earlier Supreme Court decisions that had permitted the government to limit speech that is "harmful to minors." The cases cited by the government, the Court said, provided no basis for reducing the level of First Amendment protection provided to the most participatory form of mass speech yet developed. Unlike the policies and laws upheld in those decisions, said the Court, the CDA

does not allow parents to consent to their children's use of restricted materials; is not limited to commercial transactions; fails to provide any definition of "indecent" and omits any requirement that "patently offensive" material lack socially redeeming value. 521 U.S. at 845.

Further, the Court majority wrote, the "CDA's vagueness undermines the likelihood that it has been carefully tailored to the Congressional goal of protecting minors from potentially harmful materials," adding that

[t]he CDA lacks the precision that the First Amendment requires when a statute regulates the content of speech. Although the Government has an interest in protecting children from potentially harmful materials . . . , the CDA pursues that interest by suppressing a large amount of speech that adults have a constitutional right to send and receive. Its breadth is wholly unprecedented. The CDA's burden on adult speech is unacceptable if less restrictive alternatives would be at least as effective in achieving the Act's legitimate purposes. The Government has not proved otherwise. 521 U.S. at 846.

As a matter of constitutional tradition, in the absence of evidence to the contrary, we presume that governmental regulation of the content of speech is more likely to interfere with the free exchange of ideas than to encourage it.[23]

Justice Stevens, *ACLU v. Reno II*

The Child Online Protection Act and *ACLU v. Reno III* and *IV*

Opponents of Internet censorship hailed the Supreme Court's ruling in *ACLU v. Reno II*, 521 U.S. 844 (1997), as an "overwhelming victory for Internet free speech."[28] Congressional backers of the Communications Decency Act were forced back to the drawing board to develop a statute that met the Court's concerns. In 1998 they introduced the Child Online Protection Act (COPA) (see page 109 for a copy of the law), which they hoped would survive strict scrutiny by the courts.

Signed into law on October 21, 1998, COPA makes it a federal crime to use the World Wide Web to intentionally make "any communication for commercial purposes that is available to any minor and that includes any material harmful to minors" as determined by "contemporary community standards."[29] Commercial adult Web site operators that fail to implement "reasonable measures" to prevent children from viewing such material—requiring use of a credit card, debit account, adult access code, or adult personal identification number, for example—are subject to fines as high as $50,000 for each day they are in violation of the law and up to six months in prison.

Since it applies only to commercial Web sites and employs a "harmful to minors" standard rather than the obscenity standard used in the CDA, COPA's supporters contend that it meets the objections raised by the Supreme Court in *ACLU v. Reno II*. COPA, says Bruce Taylor of the National Law Center for Children and Families, places restrictions only on commercial Web sites that are "engaged in the business of distributing material that's harmful to minors with intent to make a profit." The restrictions, he adds, do not apply to nonprofit or educational sites.

Critics charge that COPA, like the CDA, will deny users access not only to Web sites featuring hard-core pornography but also to ones with clear benefits for adults *and* young people, such as information about safer sex, contraception, and sexual harassment. "The statute," says the ACLU's Nadine Strossen, "criminalizes anything that is deemed by any community not to have serious value for minors." As a case in point, she cites the 1998 report by Special Prosecutor Kenneth Starr that detailed President Clinton's sexual relationship with White House intern Monica Lewinsky, arguing that this document might fall under COPA's "harmful to minors" prohibition despite the report's historical and political importance.

The same organizations that challenged the CDA went after the Child Online Protection Act in *ACLU v. Reno III*, 31 F. Supp 2d 473 (E.D. Pa. 1999), contending that the statute contained constitutional flaws identical to the ones that led the Supreme Court to strike down its predecessor. In February 1999, after three days of testimony, a U.S. district court issued a preliminary injunction blocking the law's enforcement because it "imposes a burden on speech that is protected for adults" *Id.*

The government's appeal of the District Court's decision also

Internet Stuck in Legal Limbo

So far the Supreme Court has determined that speech on the Internet deserves the highest level of constitutional protection. But what exactly does the "highest level of constitutional protection" mean, and will the courts continue to be so generous?

In reviewing the constitutionality of laws enacted by the federal government to regulate the media, the Supreme Court uses different standards, what it calls a "spectrum of control." To books, newspapers, pamphlets, and other written materials, the Court applies a standard called *strict scrutiny*.[24] Under this standard, a law or regulation that restricts speech will pass constitutional muster only if it serves a compelling government interest and is narrowly tailored to serve that interest: that is, it restricts free speech or freedom of the press no more than is absolutely necessary. Very few regulations subjected to this standard are found to be constitutional.

Regulations governing telephone and cable television generally are subjected to "intermediate scrutiny," which requires that they serve an important governmental interest and be substantially related to that interest in order to be judged constitutional. Some but not all federal regulations are found constitutional when this test is applied.[25]

The Court applies the third and least restrictive form of judicial review, called the "rational basis test," to television and radio. In such cases, the government must prove only that it has a legitimate interest in a particular regulation and that the measure in question is "rationally" related to that interest. Almost all regulations survive when courts look at them using this standard.[26]

In determining which forms of communication fall where they do along the Supreme Court's spectrum of control, the Court considers such factors as the number of broadcast frequencies available; how a form of communication enters the home—with or without an invitation; whether people must take affirmative steps to obtain and use the service; and whether the service is potentially pervasive—that is, whether others can watch or hear it, once it is on; and so on.

Because the Internet is not like other forms of communication, the Supreme Court in *ACLU v. Reno II* had to decide how much First Amendment protection it should receive. The Supreme Court decision (see page 51) determined that the Internet should be treated like print media and that any laws restricting it must be subjected to strict scrutiny. Yet with advances in cable, major media mergers, and the convergence of broadcast and information technologies, the Internet may soon look more like broadcasting. If the characteristics that make it unique begin to disappear, courts may reconsider whether the Internet should continue to enjoy the highest level of free speech protection.[27]

failed. In a unanimous decision in June 2000, a three-judge panel of the U.S. Court of Appeals for the Third Circuit declared COPA unconstitutional. The decision, *ACLU v. Reno IV*, 217 F.3d 162 (3d Cir. 2000), which can be found at page 77, focused chiefly on the difficulty of establishing a single "community standard" by which Internet speech could be governed:

Because of the peculiar geography-free nature of cyberspace, a "community standards" test would essentially require every Web communication to abide by the most restrictive community's standards. . . . [The overbreadth of the 1998 law] so concerns us that we are persuaded that this aspect of COPA, without reference to its other provisions, must lead inexorably to a holding of a likelihood of unconstitutionality of the entire COPA statute. 217 F.3d at 175.

On September 15, 2000, the U.S. Court of Appeals for the Third Circuit denied the federal government's request that the case be heard by the full court, not just a three-judge panel. The government on February 12, 2001, asked the U.S. Supreme Court to review the lower court's decision.[30]

How—and How Well—"Censorware" Programs Work

Advocates on both sides debate the effectiveness of filtering software, or computer programs that block access to materials on the Internet. Those who oppose governmental restriction argue that existing software is too imprecise since, along with obscenity, it screens out a lot of material that would be useful and not harmful to minors, as well as a great deal of material aimed at adults. Supporters of restrictions counter that if used correctly, current filtering software will not block protected information that is aimed at children or adults.

These filtering programs, in conjunction with a Web browser, generally work to screen out "unwanted" material online in one of three ways: (1) by blocking sites deemed inappropriate by the software manufacturer; (2) by searching the Internet for "objectionable" words and phrases and blocking sites that contain them; or (3) by allowing access only to preapproved sites.

Software vendors often will not reveal the criteria they use in deciding which sites and which keywords to block, making it impossible to monitor whether the filters actually conform to a school or library's Internet policy, to legal definitions of prohibited material—i.e., obscenity, child pornography, or material that is harmful to minors—or even to an individual user's specifications.

But the imprecision of current filtering and blocking software has produced hundreds of stories about inappropriately blocked sites. Some sites that have been blocked include: the American Red Cross, the San Diego Zoo, the Smithsonian Institution, the Declaration of Independence, the U.S. Constitution, the Bible, and the Koran. The winner of the "Foil the Filters" contest sponsored by the Digital Freedom Network in September 2000 was a high school student who was prevented from calling up his school's Web site from the school library; the library's filtering software blocked "all questionable material," including the word "high" in high school. Attempts by runner-up Hillary Anne to register hillaryanne@hotmail.com failed because censorware spotted the hidden word "aryan," which it rejected as hate speech.

In March 2001, the Consumers Union tested a number of filtering programs. Their results can be found in "Filtering Software Test: Digital Chaperones for Kids." *Consumer Reports*, Vol. 66, No. 3, p. 20, reprinted on page 140 of this book.

Restricting Internet Access in Public Libraries and Schools

Just as in homes, the Internet is rapidly becoming an essential tool for learning and communication in libraries and schools across the nation. According to a recent survey, 45 percent of Internet users rely on one of the country's nearly nine thousand public libraries for access to the Net. Some 79 percent of those libraries provide Internet access to the public.[31] A 1998 survey found that of the 89 percent of public schools connected to the Internet, 51 percent supplied access to students in classrooms, computer labs, and library media centers.[32]

Along with this proliferation has come growing concern that children whose schools and libraries provide access to the Internet will be exposed to—or will consciously look for—hard-core pornography. Those who support requiring libraries to use filtering or blocking software argue that the Internet, for all its positive educational contributions, also is "facilitating the fastest spread of the most dangerous pornography known to our society."[33] According to Enough Is Enough, a nonprofit organization that seeks to make the Internet safe for children, this spread presents two primary threats: "Children's easy access to pornography and predators' easy access to children through online chat rooms."[34]

Supporters of filtering or blocking software also object to the use of taxpayer dollars to make online pornography available to minors, and the intrusion of pornography into one of the few remaining "safe educational environments" for the nation's children. "No one expects librarians to become babysitters," says Enough Is Enough, "but parents should expect libraries (and schools) to work with them, not against them."[36]

> *Letting children use the Internet unattended, particularly talking in chat rooms, is the equivalent of dropping them off in Central Park and saying, "Go make some new friends."* [35]
>
> Enough Is Enough

The American Library Association firmly opposes limiting users' Internet access with filtering or blocking software, considering it the job of parents, not librarians to oversee children's use of the Internet.

> Parents and only parents have the right and responsibility to restrict their own children's access—and only their own children's access to library resources, including the Internet. Librarians do not serve *in loco parentis.* [37]

Surveys reveal that most librarians and library administrators share this sentiment—but not all. A number of local library boards have elected to install Internet filtering or blocking software on their computers. Like the CDA and COPA, these policies have been challenged by community members as violations of free speech.

State and federal legislative bodies have also sought to mandate the use of filtering software by public libraries. Over the past three years, at least twenty-five states have considered or passed laws mandating the use of filtering software by public libraries. In four states—Colorado, Michigan, Minnesota, and Utah—such laws are currently in place. Statutes in an additional four states—New York, Georgia, New Mexico, and Virginia—have been invalidated by federal courts as unconstitutional restrictions on free speech. [38]

In addition, in December 2000, Congress passed the Child Internet Protection Act as a rider to the budget. [39] This legislation requires schools and libraries that receive federal funds to install Internet filtering software, in order to continue qualifying for federal programs that promote universal Internet access. Concern about this measure has prompted seventeen nonprofit organizations represent-

Virginia Library Board Sued
Over Proposed Internet Restrictions

When the six branches of the Loudoun County, Virginia, library system won approval to make the Internet available to library users in 1997, the system's director asked the library board to approve a policy that provided open access for adults and for children who had their parents' permission. The board voted against the policy, calling instead for the use of Internet filtering software called X-Stop, to block "child pornography and obscene material." After negotiations failed, a local grassroots group called Mainstream Loudoun sued the library board, arguing that its Internet policy violated county residents' First Amendment right to free speech. X-Stop, the group pointed out, would block access not just to pornography but also to many sites containing valuable, constitutionally protected information, ranging from those maintained by the Safer Sex Page to those of the American Association of University Women.

The case never went to trial. In late 1998, a federal court sided with the community group and prohibited the library board from enforcing its Internet policy. Subsequently, the library board adopted the open-access Internet policy originally proposed by the system's director, with one modification—giving adults the choice to filter what they or their children look at on the Internet.

As the first decision applying free speech principles to the Internet in public libraries, this case—*Mainstream Loudoun et al. v. Board of Trustees of the Loudoun County Library et al.*, 2 F. Supp. 2d 783 (E.D. Va. 1998)—may well influence how other courts and library boards construct their Internet policies. (The opinion can be found on page 96.)

ing parents, teachers, librarians, and school administrators to urge members of Congress to drop the bill's sweeping mandatory filtering and monitoring requirements for schools and libraries. They argued:

Across the nation, communities are already working to assure that children's Internet access is properly guided. Internet use policies, innovative family educational programs, and contracts with children and families are only a few of the protective measures besides filtering software that some schools and libraries have implemented. All have made the decision based on local norms and educational philosophies and at the direction of local parents and their school and library boards.

Federal filtering mandates disregard local policymaking prerogatives [imposing instead] . . . a complex "one-size-fits-all" mandate . . . that tramples unwisely on local decision-making.[40]

But Senator John McCain (R-Ariz.), the chief U.S. Senate sponsor of school and library filtering proposals, countered: "I view it [the filtering bill] as doing for the Internet what we did for television with the V-chip. I'd like to give the people with responsibility for those schools the ability to screen out inappropriate material."[41] A new round of lawsuits by the same groups that challenged the CDA and COPA were filed in early 2001.[42] Only one thing is certain at this point: the battle will continue—in Congress, in state legislatures, and in the federal and state courts.

PART II

TRANSCRIPT OF
CLEANSPEAK:
A LOOK AT WEB CENSORSHIP
NADINE STROSSEN DEBATES
BRUCE TAYLOR

★ ★ ★ ★ ★ ★ ★ ★ ★ ★ ★ ★ ★ ★ ★ ★ ★

Nadine Strossen Debates Bruce Taylor
July 13, 1999

ANNOUNCER: From Independence Mall in Philadelphia, this is NPR's *Justice Talking*.

VOICE ONE: My eight-year-old went to a slumber party, and he came back talking about sex.com.

VOICE TWO: We have people coming into the library for the sole purpose of sexual arousal.

VOICE THREE: Librarians don't buy *Deep Throat* for their video collection. They don't put *Hustler* on the magazine rack, and they shouldn't have kids going up to a library terminal and being able to get material that includes bestiality and other kinds of materials.

VOICE FOUR: Parents need filters, but government has to help us.

VOICE FIVE: Bruce, it's intellectually dishonest to talk about obscenity and child pornography. They are already illegal; we are not opposing their censorship online.

VOICE SIX: You said that the government should not demonize hate groups. Now, what's worse, hate groups or nudity?

ANNOUNCER: Coming up on *Justice Talking*, Margot Adler hosts a debate on parents, kids, and Internet censorship. *Justice Talking* is a production of the Annenberg Public Policy Center at the University of Pennsylvania. It's recorded before a live audience in Carpenters' Hall in Philadelphia.

MARGOT ADLER: Welcome to *Justice Talking*. I'm Margot Adler. *Justice Talking* takes an in-depth look at the cases and controversies that come before our nation's courts and challenge our nation's conscience.

In this edition of *Justice Talking*, we'll visit the site of the newest free speech battle, the Internet. Freedom of expression in this country has often been tested at the margins; in fact, the Constitution runs into its most complex challenges when confronted with the most unpopular forms of speech, like pornography. The Internet has created a new frontier for this debate, by making it far easier to publish and widely distribute sexually explicit material and far more difficult to restrict access to it.

Coming up on *Justice Talking*, Online Porn, a debate between the ACLU's Nadine Strossen and Bruce Taylor of the National Law Center for Children and Families. First, this background report on legislative attempts to police cyberspace from NPR's Larry Abramson.

LARRY ABRAMSON: When it comes to the Internet, Congress has been pulled in many directions. Right now, there's a loud call to keep hands off of the new medium for fear that any regulations will slow the growth of the information economy. But at the same time, lawmakers have been sorely tempted to regulate online content. The first law was the Communications Decency Act, a bold stroke that sought to ban all indecent material on the Internet. The Supreme Court struck down that law in 1997 before it ever went into effect, calling it too broad, too likely to trammel on the free speech rights of people who might publish on the Net, which is to say everyone on the planet. In 1998 Congress took another stab; for Ohio congressman Michael Oxley of the House Commerce Committee, there's simply no reason for different laws for on- and offline images.

MICHAEL OXLEY: The bookstores that sell this kind of material, in most cases, by local ordinance or state law, are banned from having that material out in a window where children can pass by and see it. Adults who want to buy this information or this pornographic material have every constitutional right to do so, but the stores cannot simply provide it in the window.

ABRAMSON: Oxley's efforts in the last Congress helped pass the Child Online Protection Act, or COPA. This time, Congress sought to fashion a narrow law that would survive court scrutiny. It only required that users show some form of online ID before they could see material defined as "harmful to minors." But in the boundless confines of the Internet, many saw COPA as a direct threat.

WOMAN: Welcome to the lesbian rights summit.

ABRAMSON: This is a cybercast from PlanetOut, a gay and lesbian Web page. PlanetOut joined a coalition of online publishers to sue the government over COPA. They argued that someone, somewhere, might decide their content was harmful to minors. The publishers would then be required to ask for online proof of age, often a credit card, which they said would scare away people who turned to the Web for anonymous advice.

LOWELL REED: Resuming the second day of the preliminary injunction hearing in the matter of ACLU and others versus Reno, civil action 98-5591 . . .

ABRAMSON: The suit landed in the lap of Federal Judge Lowell Reed in Philadelphia. Attorneys for the American Civil Liberties Union argued that requiring proof of age for certain material was unworkable. PlanetOut's Thomas P. Reilly testified that the law would require that publishers anticipate what might be considered harmful to minors in order to avoid prosecution.

ATTORNEY: Do you understand which community standards would be used to judge what material is harmful to minors?

THOMAS P. REILLY: Well, it's very interesting. We operate a community of interests rather than a community of geography. So our members live all over the world, including in the United States. And we have community, and by our community standards, none of the information on our site is offensive in any way. However, there are communities of geography, such as small towns in, let's say, Biloxi, Mississippi, where I'm not sure that they would agree, that they would apply their community standards to us in a way that we would not agree with.

ABRAMSON: The plaintiffs won round one when Judge Reed handed down a preliminary injunction and the suit recently survived an appeal, and that's kept the law in check. COPA and the Communications Decency Act showed how difficult it is to design legislative restrictions on material viewed in private, but many feel the government has a far more compelling interest when the computers are paid for with public funds.

In Loudoun County, Virginia, in 1998, the local library board found itself in the national spotlight when a federal court struck down its policy on Internet filtering. Filters can screen out objectionable material online, and the library board had required that all library computers throughout the county be equipped with software that could block porn. When a federal court ruled that policy was unconstitutional, citizens debated at a public meeting whether to spend more of their tax dollars on an appeal.

WOMAN: The First Amendment was never intended to protect obscene speech, much less images of violent sexual acts involving not only children but animals and nonconsenting women. Yet it is precisely this type of material that plaintiffs Mainstream Loudoun et al. would force Loudoun taxpayers to provide access to on county library computer terminals.

MAN: Censorship is an ugly thing. Pornography is an ugly thing, but censorship is much more dangerous than pornography ever could be. How dare anyone come up here and suggest that they are in a position of moral or intellectual superiority, so as to be in a position to deny another adult the right to read and peruse whatever they please? That is not only Yugoslavia, that is totalitarian dictatorship no matter where it is.

ABRAMSON: In the end, the board decided not to appeal and took the filters off. This debate continues in communities around the country. Some have devised compromises to avoid court battles, like privacy screens, so patrons won't be forced to look at risqué material that people might call up on library computers. These halfway measures have not satisfied people like Karen Jo Gounaud of Family Friendly Libraries. She feels that requiring filters only for some computers ignores a key point.

KAREN JO GOUNAUD: We have people coming into the library for the sole purpose of sexual arousal. So what you now have going on in libraries that you didn't before is extensive sexual activity of that nature that used to only occasionally be seen in a bathroom by a guy off the street.

ABRAMSON: Right now, the federal government provides more than $2 billion in annual subsidies for Internet connections in libraries and schools, and many politicians are concerned that without mandatory filters, those computers imply government endorsement of reckless surfing. Republican Senator John McCain has introduced a bill that will require Internet filters for federally funded Internet connections in schools and libraries.

JOHN MCCAIN: No issue is more important to America than protecting our children. The Internet holds unlimited opportunities to inform and educate. Unfortunately, there are those who would use this new technology for purposes harmful to our kids. This bill is not a panacea, and it can't replace the importance of teacher and parent involvement. What it can do is to provide a baseline of protection for our children.

ABRAMSON: The steady flow of new laws in this area has helped galvanize civil liberties groups. Many of them see the Internet as the key battleground for free speech issues and are dead set against any restrictions on content. At the same time, growing concern over pornography and violence online is attracting conservative groups who feel that ground rules for responsible speech must be set down, while the Internet is still young.

For *Justice Talking*, I'm Larry Abramson reporting.

ADLER: Do laws aimed at protecting children from online pornography work? Are they constitutional, or do they infringe on the rights of adults to obtain controversial materials? This is *Justice Talking*, and I'm Margot Adler. We are joined today by two experienced advocates.

Nadine Strossen is the president of the American Civil Liberties Union. She is the first woman to head the nation's oldest and largest civil liberties organization, a position she's held since 1991. Nadine Strossen is a professor of law at New York Law School, a regular columnist for the Webzine intellectualcapital.com, and the author of *Defending Pornography, Free Speech, Sex and the Fight for Women's Rights.*

Bruce Taylor is president and chief counsel of the National Law Center for Children and Families, based in Fairfax, Virginia. Mr. Taylor has spent the last twenty-five years prosecuting hundreds of obscenity cases and appeals, most recently as a senior trial attorney for the Child Exploitation and Obscenity Section of the U.S. Department of Justice. A former prosecutor for the city of Cleveland, Ohio, Mr. Taylor argued the celebrated case *Larry Flynt v. Ohio* before the U.S. Supreme Court in 1981.

It's good to have you both here. We're going to start our discussion with opening statements from our guests, beginning with Nadine Strossen of the ACLU.

NADINE STROSSEN: Thank you, Margot. I'm delighted to participate in your wonderful show. I'm very happy to say that my position on these issues is not just the one that is endorsed by the American Civil Liberties Union and other cyberlibertarians. It's also the position that has been endorsed by the entire United States Supreme Court in its landmark ruling in *Reno v. ACLU*, striking down the Communications Decency Act.

Specifically, the Court held there that the Internet should receive the highest degree of First Amendment protection, which the print media has long enjoyed. Because of its unique accessibility and interactivity, the Internet makes it possible for all mature individuals to make our own choices about what material to look at and what not to, and also to make our own choices about what our own children should see or not see. In short, all individuals and all families can act autonomously, consistent with their own values, their own beliefs, and their own interests. As I'm fond of saying, the ACLU is a profamily organization. We just don't think that the American family includes Big Brother as a member.

Reno v. ACLU struck down the CDA because it restricted adults' free speech rights, but there are also additional reasons for opposing Internet censorship based on the rights not of adults, but on the rights of young people themselves. Much of the sexually oriented expression that has been targeted by these Internet censorship laws, far from harming young people, to the contrary is positively beneficial for them—for example, information about safer sex, contraception, and sexual harassment. So Internet censorship laws are no better for young people's welfare than they are for adults' free speech rights, and Judge Reed made precisely that point in striking down COPA. As he concluded, "[P]erhaps we do the minors of this country more harm than good if First Amendment rights, which they will, with age, inherit fully, are chipped away in the name of their protection."

ADLER: Thank you, the ACLU's Nadine Strossen. Now, Bruce Taylor, your opening statement.

BRUCE TAYLOR: When Judge Reed, of the Federal District Court in Philadelphia, issued his preliminary injunction against the Child Online Protection Act, what struck me most about his opinion was not that he made it, because we could see from the hearing that he was apparently buying into the arguments made by the plaintiffs who were on the stand, giving the Judge their heartfelt fears that somehow this new law that came out of Congress that said that commercial Web pages that regularly sell pornography that's harmful to minors must take a credit card or a PIN number or some identifier before they show free samples of that harmful matter. And they said, "This is going to be aimed at me, Your Honor, and all I do is have information on my Web site about sexual health practices for handicapped people; I can't put any information out there that some people in Biloxi, Mississippi, or some redneck prosecutor in Kansas is going to jump up and grab me for."

We argued that the judge had the duty to construe and interpret the statute so that that couldn't happen, and that judge didn't do that when he issued the preliminary injunction. He said kids can take care of themselves and it's better for them to have an unrestricted First Amendment when they grow up than it is to have laws for their protection while they are still minors. Children have a lot of desires to do a lot of things that parents don't want them to do, but that doesn't mean we let them do it. When they get big enough and they can make their own laws, maybe they will change everything. But that doesn't mean that we're going to abandon all efforts to try to make this Internet something that children can turn on in the home, in the school, in their library, go surf in the Web, use the search engine, and ask for *boys*, *girls*, *toys*, *boy scouts*, *actresses*, or *cheerleader* and not get a hundred hot links to hardcore porn sites that will show free pictures to those kids as soon as they click on one of those red lines of text. That's the purpose of COPA. It says, If you're in the business of selling pornography, take your credit card before you show the free teasers. If you want to sell adult material, then sell adult material to adults. I think that those two concepts of the law, saying we're going to put restrictions on the pornographers and not put restrictions on serious sexual speech, can coexist, and I hope for that reason that the ACLU loses the lawsuit and that the Judge's order is reversed.

ADLER: Thank you, Bruce Taylor. You're listening to *Justice Talking*. Our debate on free speech, pornography, and the Internet continues after this short break.

ANNOUNCER: Surfing the Web? Point your browser to the *Justice Talking* Web site at www.justicetalking.org. You can listen to all of our programs, read about our guests, and find links to more information about the hot issues we're debating. That's www.justice talking.org.

ADLER: Welcome back to *Justice Talking*. I'm Margot Adler. We're joined by one of our nation's leading crusaders for free speech, Nadine Strossen, of the American Civil Liberties Union, and one of our nation's leading crusaders against pornography, Bruce Taylor, of the National Law Center for Children and Families. You helped design the law that we're discussing, Bruce. How have you tried to answer the Supreme Court's concerns?

TAYLOR: One of the interesting things about the CDA case, the first one that went to the Supreme Court, was that the Justices, when they announced the CDA decision, said that the Internet should be entitled to the same First Amendment rights as the print medium enjoys. And because of that, Congress went back, when they designed COPA, and looked at what laws apply in the states and under the federal codes to the print medium, meaning magazines, videos, and other photographic types of depictions of sexual activity that we would normally call pornography. COPA then said it will be limited to commercial sites on the Web and not apply to nonprofit or educational sites. So it doesn't apply to the .edu or .org organizations because they're not commercial sites. It also applies only to those sites that are engaged in the business of distributing material that's harmful to minors with intent to make a profit.

ADLER: I'm sure you'd like to respond to this, Nadine.

STROSSEN: Bruce, I'm disappointed to hear that you actually participated in drafting the statute, because you have proven yourself to be an extraordinarily poor draftsman. If you match Bruce's description of what the statute purportedly does against the statute's language, you would see a world of difference. Judge Reed, who took pains to express his sympathy with the goals that Bruce has espoused here, nevertheless said those goals are not what is served by this statute. It is not limited only to those who are, to quote Bruce, "in the business of selling pornography." It doesn't matter that these discussions have serious value, because the statute criminalizes anything that is deemed by any community not to have serious value for minors. Let me cite a recent case in point. The Starr report, which was put up on the Internet instantaneously, I believe even before it was available in hard copy so to speak, was immediately censored by filtering software in public schools all across the country, and the statutory language expressly says, contrary to Bruce's oral description of it, that you will fall under the statute if you put online any communication that includes any material that is harmful to minors. For that reason, the Judge agreed with us that this law is making criminals not just of the Larry Flynts of the world, not just of Nadine Strossen and the ACLU, but also these other nefarious pornographers: the American Booksellers Association, MSNBC, *Time* magazine, and the *New York Times, Philadelphia Gay News.*

ADLER: Nadine, I want to ask Bruce, would minors be restricted in reading the Starr report under COPA?

TAYLOR: Absolutely not, and I'm surprised that Nadine Strossen, who is a lawyer, and I understand she's a law professor, doesn't know or won't admit to a little more of the interpretation of the legal test, because it's not what someone thinks is harmful to minors or someone thinks has value. "Harmful to minors," like obscenity, is a legal test, and the Supreme Court has said what limits are on that. And as a matter of fact, when the Starr report was issued, there were members of Congress and the committee report that pointed out that the Starr report could not be harmful to minors under COPA for two reasons: one, its serious political value cannot be denied. Even if you thought it had no artistic or literary or scientific value, you couldn't deny that it has political value. But the other reason that the Starr report would not be in violation of COPA is that the types of sexual descriptions in the Starr report are not the kind that you'd find in *Penthouse* or *Playboy* or *Hustler* where they describe, in prurient detail, the kind of sexual activity that we normally call pornography and that the courts have said "harmful to minors" laws apply to.

ADLER: My eight-year-old, Nadine, went to a slumber party just about a month ago, and he came back talking about sex.com. And I happen to know that he can go online, and I let him go online; I don't have any filtering software yet, and he can click on *pet*, *toy*, *girl*, and sexually explicit sites are going to come up. I'm—I feel uncomfortable about this. What do you say?

STROSSEN: What I say to you, Margot, is what the American Library Association experts who deal with children's literature say about traditional kinds of literature: there is no substitute for parental judgment. The very best kind of filtering device is a parent training a child to make critical judgments about what information is useful and not useful.

ADLER: But in our society that's not there all the time.

STROSSEN: Well, it's not there all the time for any kind of medium. And ask yourself, would I allow the kinds of restrictions that are being advocated for the Net for other kinds of media?

ADLER: Well, let's go in the other direction. How do you think seeing sexually explicit materials harms children? Bruce.

TAYLOR: Children are gonna be harmed in the sense that the whole purpose of pornography is not to give a message about sexuality, it's to sell dirty pictures to guys, basically, and kids aren't ready for that kind of material. I don't think adult men are ready for that kind of material. But parents have the right to say no pornographer has the right to show that stuff to my kid until my kid is old enough to make his or her own opinion about that. And, we ask storekeepers to put the *Playboy*s and the *Penthouse*s and the *Hustler*s under the counter. And we ask TV stations and radio stations not to have that kind of adult material on the air when kids are in the audience. Then that's what the law should do with the Internet.

ADLER: Nadine, do you think there is any harm in children seeing sexually explicit material?

STROSSEN: I think, in the abstract, the answer to that is no. It all depends on the context. First of all, what is the material? The government didn't even bother to put in any evidence about any harm from any of the material that was banned by these laws. Conversely, the ACLU put in evidence that a lot of the material that is outlawed by these statutes would be affirmatively beneficial because it provides information as well as educational resources for children.

ADLER: Bruce, is something that's harmful to a six-year-old the same as something that's harmful to an eleven-year-old, or a sixteen-year-old adolescent who's questioning his or her sexuality?

TAYLOR: Well, again, one of the good things about this law, COPA, in particular, uses the "harmful to minors" test, which has been interpreted by the courts, including the federal courts and the state courts and the U.S. Supreme Court, to apply to the age group to which the material is aimed, so that you don't judge whether something is harmful to six-year-olds, when the audience that it went to was a group of sixteen-year-olds, whether it's—

STROSSEN: But, Bruce, the Internet doesn't draw age distinctions. By definition, any material that is online anywhere is available to anybody of any age whatsoever. So if you win your case, it means that adults of the highest age level, as well as the youngest minors, are going to be deprived of access to all of this material.

TAYLOR: Except that if we win the case, COPA won't apply to any of the material that you have discussed. Your Web site won't be censored. The ObGyn and the PlanetOut, none of that kind of material that has serious discussions of sex, even if controversial, comes within this statute.

ANNOUNCER: You're listening to *Justice Talking*, a debate on pornography, free speech, and the Internet. Arguing for tighter legislative restriction of the Internet is Bruce Taylor of the National Law Center for Children and Families.

TAYLOR: We hated a lot of the things that Big Brother, and now it's Big Sister, may want to impose on us, but that doesn't mean that we're going to abandon all efforts to try to make this Internet something that children can turn on and not get a hundred hot links to hard-core porn sites.

ANNOUNCER: Opposed is Nadine Strossen, president of the ACLU.

STROSSEN: The Internet makes it possible for all mature individuals to make our own choices about what our own children should see or not see, rather than having the government impose uniform standards on all of us.

ANNOUNCER: *Justice Talking* continues with your host, Margot Adler.

ADLER: At this point I'd like to ask each of you to pose a question to your opponent. First, Bruce Taylor, your question for Nadine Strossen.

TAYLOR: Nadine, if you were defense attorney for one of the plaintiffs in your case, PlanetOut, SeeNet, your own Web site, or the Sexual Health Network, would you argue that your client's material was "harmful to minors," or would you argue that none of the test of the "harmful to minors" standard applies, meaning that it's not prurient, it's not offensive, and it has serious value for minors? And if so, why don't you just take the tack that none of this material is threatened by COPA and let the COPA law apply to the pornography it was intended to?

STROSSEN: Bruce, unfortunately, COPA is written in a far more broad way than you have described it. On its face, it clearly extends to material that, on the whole, is greatly valuable because, as I said earlier, any portion of even a very long document that includes a small fraction that could be considered harmful to minors in any particular community is going to make the entire document or the entire image illegal. I think the only honest definition we've ever had of any kind of obscenity from the Supreme Court is Potter Stewart's famous dictum when he said, "I cannot define it, but I know it when I see it." And that subjective open-ended nature of this so-called definition means anything with any sexual content is endangered.

ADLER: Now, Nadine Strossen, your question for Bruce Taylor.

STROSSEN: Well, Bruce, I know that you consider yourself to be a conservative, and I understand conservatives to be very keen on reducing the role of government in our private lives, getting the government out of our living room, out of our bedroom. Why then are you supporting laws that are inserting the government into the most intimate aspects of our lives, our homes, and our decisions about how we raise our own children?

TAYLOR: I guess the easy answer to that is because I don't hate my government, and my difference with you is that I interpret COPA narrowly so that it's not unconstitutional, and you interpret it so broadly that it is.

ADLER: We'd like to now go into the audience and get some comments and questions.

MAN: This is a question for Bruce Taylor. I agree with you that the difference between you and Nadine Strossen seems to be on how broadly the law would be interpreted. But if you think about the history of prosecutors looking at books, it does seem that the history is that prosecutors have tended to interpret such laws broadly and to go after exactly the kinds of materials that you think prosecutors would not go after. So my question is, if you look at the history of censorship of book publication, doesn't that support Nadine's side?

TAYLOR: Not anymore. And one of the good things about using the "harmful to minors" test it was upheld by the Supreme Court in 1968. Since that time, since the *Ginsberg* test in '68, since the *Miller* decision in '73, all of the prosecutions in this country have been against what we call hard-core pornography, and that's why you can say with some confidence, "harmful to minors" laws have only been used against pornographic material, and that's the only limit that the courts have upheld. And obscenity laws have only been used against hard-core pornography, and that's what the courts have drawn the limits for.

STROSSEN: Well that's absolutely untrue, as a matter of fact, and Bruce, I'm happy to give you citations afterward. But the Starr report, in fact, has been censored as supposedly "harmful to minors—"

TAYLOR: But not found "harmful to minors."

STROSSEN: *Our Bodies, Ourselves* has been attacked. The Bible has been attacked because of its sexualized violence. Bruce's argument essentially comes down to the same argument that was made in both of our Internet censorship cases that the judges squarely rejected, namely prosecutors saying, "Trust us to enforce the law narrowly." And Judge, Chief Judge of the Third Circuit, Dolores Slovitor said prosecutors come and go, even federal judges are limited to life tenure. The First Amendment remains to give protection to future generations as well. The "trust us" argument just won't fly.

ADLER: Nadine, does the government have any interest in banning obscene material in any form?

STROSSEN: Well, we have not challenged the obscenity aspects of these laws. The extent to which they simply carry forward the prohibition on obscenity that has been upheld in traditional media to the Internet, we have not challenged that. In point of fact, though, I do think the obscenity exception to the First Amendment is a very questionable one, and I'm in very good company. It has been questioned by many Supreme Court Justices, including Antonin Scalia, who is hardly a radical leftist. But he recognizes that the definition of obscenity, if that's what you can call it, is so subjective that, in effect, it gives unfettered discretion to prosecutors, judges, and juries to go after whatever material with any sexual content they don't like.

ADLER: So where do you draw the line—

STROSSEN: I draw the line—

ADLER: —snuff films, child pornography, bestiality, what?

STROSSEN: No. It's very, very easy to draw the line suggested by raising the question of child pornography. Child pornography, as it's traditionally been recognized in this country, involves sexual material that is produced by using actual children in the production: an unconsenting, immature individual who is being exploited and, therefore, a living human being who is harmed in the production process. That is a completely different type of harm from the asserted harm that Bruce is basing his arguments on, namely, the harm, supposedly, to somebody's mind from seeing an image or reading a text that might cause a nasty idea to arise in that person's mind.

ADLER: Bruce, where do you personally draw the line?

TAYLOR: Well, that's been easy for me because I don't draw one myself and I don't try to rewrite the law like Nadine said. Nadine's position is that of the ACLU, which says that it may be criminal to use a child to make child porn, to abuse a kid, but once the pedophile has made the picture, he can sell it from his jail cell because even child porn, like obscenity, like harmful matter, is constitutionally protected. I think the law does a great job. I'm just not trying to repeal them all like the ACLU is.

ADLER: Let's go on to more questions from the audience.

MAN: Bruce, speaking about drawing the line, if you're protecting children against pornography, would you also protect them against racially offensive material, or hate propaganda, or ethnically offensive material?

TAYLOR: If I had a vote, I would like to do something to protect children from some of the hate and the violent kind of material on the Internet. Under present law that's not illegal and it's protected speech under the First Amendment to hate everyone and to talk about it all you want. However, one of the good things that was put into the Communications Decency Act three years ago were civil immunity protections for private industry. In other words, Congress enabled the Internet service providers like AOL or CompuServe or Prodigy to voluntarily block access on their own servers to the Nazis or the Klan or to some of the more violent or even pornographic material.

STROSSEN: You accept, Bruce, the voluntary actions either by private sector companies or by individual parents and families with respect to any kind of content that a particular family might consider to be offensive or inappropriate for a particular child. But you want the government to step in and take that discretion away from individuals and families only when it comes to material with sexual content.

ADLER: You're listening to *Justice Talking*, and we're talking about sexually explicit material on the World Wide Web. Are laws aimed at limiting children's exposure to these words and images constitutional, or do these policies violate the First Amendment? More of our debate after this short break.

ADLER: This is *Justice Talking*. I'm Margot Adler. We wanted to know what the public thinks about censorship and the Internet, and what public opinion surveys are saying about it, so we invited public opinion research analyst Ethel Klein, president of EDK Associates, to clue us in.

ETHEL KLEIN: What you'll find [is] that, overall, people think the Internet's a great thing. You'll also find that a lot of people don't know what it is, but they get a sense that it's the sign of progress. It's the way of making the world smaller. It's a way of bringing us together, and that mostly it has done good things. They worry about access to information mostly for children, and what children can see and get to without parental supervision. And that's where they want something done. I mean, if you ask them, they'll tell you that the Internet providers don't exert enough influence on making sure that sites that are inappropriate for children are not available to them.

On the one hand, if you ask them, Should there be more stringent guidelines on the Internet? the answer is absolutely yes. You get consensus on that. But when you ask them, What's the real problem? they'll tell you its lack of parental supervision. Their second answer is to have the industry regulate itself, and their third answer is to have government do it.

ADLER: This issue seems to back up against the old American belief in freedom, and it also connects to people's fear of the new and strange, doesn't it?

KLEIN: It certainly backs up into people's sense of new and strange, and those who champion new and strange love it. I think the Luddites amongst us are stuck because, on some level, the general culture says this is a very good thing. On the other hand, they think all technology brings with it some unexpected and undesired consequences, and they point to this as one of the real dangers. Now people will say that, in just the same way that we regulate print materials, we should be able to regulate the Internet. The problem is, the Internet is not the same as print materials. It's a more complicated thing. It takes you into many more layers, many more worlds. It's much harder to really supervise in any kind of way. And I think what people are afraid of is that it's their sense of being out of control, and parents do worry that they will be out of control once their kids enter.

Also I think the other thing that, really, the Internet is bumping into is people's privacy fears. In fact, if you were to ask me to name the one thing that they're most afraid of, is what the Internet does for privacy issues, and that's one of the reasons they haven't been able to use it as a commercial vehicle as well as they'd had liked. People are very concerned about access to all this information about them. This is a major intrusion into their home. They worry when they hear about these viruses entering their data stream, because it means that things can come in and out without them knowing about it or having any control over it. And, you know, there are all these movies now about how we're all going to be wired together and be controlled, and a lot of people worry that that could come true.

ADLER: Ethel, thanks for joining us. Ethel Klein is president of EDK Associates.

ADLER: Welcome back to *Justice Talking*, where Nadine Strossen of the ACLU and Bruce Taylor of the National Law Center for Children and Families are debating free speech and cyberporn. We'd like to go back into the audience and take your questions.

WOMAN: I have a question for Mr. Taylor. Mr. Taylor, recently at the Pennsylvania Psychological Association meeting, they called the Internet the new crack cocaine. There were very troubling discussions about the new and provocative research about the extremely negative impact of pornography on brain response. That in fact showing pornography to children meets the criteria for child sexual abuse, and anyone with a charge card could do it. It's just illegal for a child to do it on their own.

TAYLOR: Well, one of the things that has to be kept in mind is that COPA is only one of the federal or state laws that are designed to protect children. COPA merely says that if material is harmful to minors, that a commercial Web site has to take an adult identifier before showing that harmful material. So if a child were to steal Dad's credit card or Dad's PIN number, then they could get into those Web sites. Right now the problem is those Web sites aren't under any control. You go to the first page of sex.com or whitehouse.com or nasa.com or pokemon.com, and there's porn pictures.

STROSSEN: This question points out Judge Reed's conclusion that this law is as ineffective in achieving its asserted purpose of shielding kids from certain online material as it is violative of the free speech rights of adults.

TAYLOR: And, too, ten-year-olds don't have credit cards. It's more like high school or college age, older teens.

ADLER: We have some young people here, actually.

BOY: I have two questions. My first one is, what's wrong with sex anyway? Why demonize sex? I mean, child porn and things like that are already banned. And my second question is, you said that the government should not demonize hate groups, but it should demonize nudity. Now, what's worse, hate groups or nudity?

TAYLOR: And those are good questions. And one of the answers is, there's nothing wrong with sex, and hopefully parents would expect their kids would grow up with a healthy attitude toward sex. Most adults feel that pornography doesn't give that kind of an attitude. Nudity isn't obscene, and nudity isn't "harmful to minors." Hard-core pornography is obscene, and soft-core pornography, like *Playboy*, is "harmful to minors" because it doesn't give that same kind of message that sex is good that you were assuming.

STROSSEN: Now Bruce, again, you're describing the statute very differently from the way it is written, because it does define as prohibited sexual conduct any nudity or indeed partial nudity, including even showing the bare breasts of a postpubescent female. So nudity is deemed "harmful to minors," and I couldn't agree more with the young questioner that I think that kind of attitude about the dangerousness of nudity and sexuality is itself harmful to minors.

ADLER: Let's go back into the audience for some more comments and questions.

MAN: Bruce, as a conservative, why haven't you and others like you put your efforts into developing effective filtering devices, making those devices freely available so that individuals and individual families can make their own decisions about whether to censor sexual content or violence or hate material? Isn't it really fundamentally that you want the government to make those decisions for families or individuals who may not agree with you?

TAYLOR: To some extent, I think, it's a combination of what government and parents and industry should have to do. I have been a big proponent, for the past three years, of parents using filters. And as a matter of fact, I try to be somewhat of an alarmist only on that subject by saying, if you're a parent and you've got a teenager and you got an Internet connection, your kid has already seen materials that are so hard core that that Mafia wouldn't sell them in Times Square bookstores. And so you better use filters. And I do think parents should have a filter, and they should set them. And schools should have them, and I even think libraries should have filters to filter out some of the child pornography and the hardcore obscenity. Librarians don't buy *Deep Throat* for their video collection. They don't put *Hustler* on the magazine rack, and they shouldn't have kids going up to a library terminal and being able to get material that . . . includes not only that but bestiality and other kinds of material.

ADLER: Nadine, what about libraries? They don't stock *Hustler*; they don't stock pornography. Why shouldn't they have some regulation of this?

STROSSEN: The libraries have applied the same standards online as they have traditionally applied to books. Rather than denying access to material, being very aggressive in educating kids and parents about how to take the maximum advantage out of this marvelous new resource, putting out lists of Web sites that are particularly recommended for kids of particular ages. The American Library Association has always had the position that access to library materials should never be denied or restricted on the basis of age.

ADLER: I'd like to, before we end this program, get a few brief comments from the audience. Just a few statements.

MAN: After listening to both of you tonight, I have come to the opinion that I don't like even the amount of censorship we have now. I'm deathly afraid of what that can grow to. I think the only answer is for a parent to, by his or her example, show their children and grandchildren what their morality is and what they believe in, and to have the child act similarly.

WOMAN: Okay, you've each put forth two really different positions tonight that you characterize as perfectly fine choices or positions. I think a lot of us see only flawed choices. So I'm curious if each of you sees a downside to your own choice?

ADLER: I like that question so much that I think that instead of going on, I'd love to hear the response to each of these, yes.

STROSSEN: I agree that it's flawed insofar as you could say our choices come down to (1) trust individuals and individual parents, and I understand that not all parents and not all individuals are perfect. They're not going to make perfectly responsible decisions with respect to their children. But on the other hand, the other flawed alternative that Bruce is offering is, trust the government, trust prosecutors. You know, they're both flawed. But I think I would rather put my faith and my trust in individuals and parents rather than in the government.

ADLER: Bruce.

TAYLOR: And that's a good question. When I think of where could I go wrong, if everything I've advocated came true, and one of the things I'd be afraid of is that people would misunderstand the law and maybe prosecutors or judges wouldn't follow the law even if prosecutors were trying to. I just would rather err on the side of protecting the children than to take the stand that I'm afraid to do anything.

MAN: As both a parent and a minister, I don't trust the ACLU or the American Library Association any more than I trust the government. Why should I trust those groups and presume that you have my best interest at heart? You people deal in a theoretical level. You don't deal with the young people that are hurt by this that I have seen and have had to deal with. And I think it's about time you come down to the real world and deal with people and the harm that is done and the victims of pornography.

MAN: Three years ago I asked my then twelve-year-old son whether or not he thought it would be appropriate for us to buy blocking materials for the Internet. And he looked at me, and he said, "Daddy, I went online a year ago and blocked pornography because I didn't think we should have it in our house." And my comment is, I wouldn't have known how to keep it out. He knew how to keep it out or how to keep it in and, in the real world, your best conservative values are raising children who can make those judgments as early as the age of eleven, as my son did. You are living in a fool's paradise if you think that the government, especially this government with all of its inefficiencies, is as good as my bright, now fifteen-year-old son.

ADLER: Our time together is coming to an end. I'd like to ask both Nadine Strossen and Bruce Taylor to make their closing statements. First, Nadine.

STROSSEN: Thank you, Margot. The ACLU has always been a non-partisan organization, since support for or opposition to civil liberty's principles crosses all party and ideological lines, and citizens who oppose cybercensorship include not only liberal advocates of free speech but also conservative advocates of limited government. I'd like to end by sharing one of my favorite e-mails ever which illustrates this point. I got it from a member of the Christian Coalition after she'd seen me on TV debating Ralph Reed, who was then the Christian Coalition's executive director, on cybercensorship. But she agreed with my position on this issue. She wrote, "Dear Nadine Strossen: I am a mother of two, Christian, pro-lifer. I have very rarely agreed with the ACLU until now. I saw you on *Crossfire*. You know what you were talking about. I don't like pornographic material or some of the other speech on the net, but the First Amendment says that it can be there just as much as I can. The Internet is like cable. If you don't want it, don't subscribe to it. If you do, but don't want the kids to see all of it, then get a filtering program. It is my responsibility to take care of my kids, not the government's." She then ends by quoting one of my favorite lines from Voltaire, and I think it's appropriate before I hand the mike over to Bruce: "I may not agree with you, but I will defend to the death your right to say it."

ADLER: Thank you, Nadine. And now a closing statement from Bruce.

TAYLOR: It was also said that you are what you eat, and unfortunately not all of the children who consume pornography or the hate and violence on the Internet are going to be as mature and kind-hearted and wise as the ones who would know enough to block it off. The children all know that this material is there. And what American law is hopefully going to do is to put some restrictions on the worst kinds of material that are illegal in the real world and extend those to the Internet so that kids won't have to be kept off; so that parents won't have to use filters; so even if you have a filter at your house, you're not going to worry about your kid going next door or to the school or to the public library and downloading this kind of material.

I think we need to, in a sense, grow up and act like the Internet is just another means of communication. Consenting adults don't have the right under the First Amendment to obtain obscenity. Adults don't have the right to sell material that's "harmful to minors" to a child of someone else's. And you don't have a right to make child pornography, even of your own kids. Those laws are part of our fabric, and if you don't like them, you can go to a country maybe that doesn't have those kind of laws. But as long as we, as a society, think those are a good restriction to put on those people who don't know right from wrong, then those laws should be available on the Internet, so that we don't have to keep our kids from the Internet. And that those of us who maybe aren't as techno-savvy, or if I'm an immigrant, or if I don't speak English, or if I'm a working parent and I want my kid to use the Internet, I'm not going to have to worry about some other person, a pornographer or a pedophile, having access to my kid, just so that my kid can have access to the Internet.

ADLER: Thank you, Bruce. I want to thank our audience and our guests, Bruce Taylor of the National Law Center for Children and Families and Nadine Strossen of the ACLU.

And finally, we close tonight's program with this very appropriate thought, a quote from Supreme Court Justice William Brennan. He wrote:

Current Justices read the Constitution in the only way that we can: as twentieth-century Americans. We look to the history of the time of framing and to the intervening history of interpretation. But the ultimate question must be: What do the words of the text mean in our time? For the genius of the Constitution rests not in any static meaning it may have had in a world that is dead and gone, but in the adaptability of its great principles to cope with current problems and current needs. Our Constitution was not intended to preserve a preexisting society, but to make a new one.

I'm Margot Adler. Thanks for listening to *Justice Talking*.

(Children reciting "We, the people . . .")

PART III

PRIMARY SOURCES

AMERICAN CIVIL LIBERTIES UNION ET AL. V. RENO II

No. 96-511

SUPREME COURT OF THE UNITED STATES

521 U.S. 844; 117 S. Ct. 2329; 1997 U.S. LEXIS 4037; 138 L. Ed. 2d 874

March 19, 1997, Argued

June 26, 1997, Decided

PRIOR HISTORY:
On appeal from the United States District Court for the Eastern District of Pennsylvania, reported at: 929 F. Supp. 824 (1996)

DISPOSITION:
929 F. Supp. 824, *affirmed.*

SYLLABUS:
Two provisions of the Communications Decency Act of 1996 (CDA or Act) seek to protect minors from harmful material on the Internet, an international network of interconnected computers that enables millions of people to communicate with one another in "cyberspace" and to access vast amounts of information from around the world. Title 47 U.S.C.A. § 223(a)(1)(B)(ii) (Supp. 1997) criminalizes the "knowing" transmission of "obscene or indecent" messages to any recipient under 18 years of age. Section 223(d) prohibits the "knowing" sending or displaying to a person under 18 of any message "that, in context, depicts or describes, in terms patently offensive as measured by contemporary community standards, sexual or excretory

activities or organs." Affirmative defenses are provided for those who take "good faith, . . . effective . . . actions" to restrict access by minors to the prohibited communications, § 223(e)(5)(A), and those who restrict such access by requiring certain designated forms of age proof, such as a verified credit card or an adult identification number, § 223(e)(5)(B). A number of plaintiffs filed suit challenging the constitutionality of §§ 223(a)(1) and 223(d). After making extensive findings of fact, a three-judge District Court convened pursuant to the Act entered a preliminary injunction against enforcement of both challenged provisions. The court's judgment enjoins the Government from enforcing § 223(a)(1)(B)'s prohibitions insofar as they relate to "indecent" communications, but expressly preserves the Government's right to investigate and prosecute the obscenity or child pornography activities prohibited therein. The injunction against enforcement of § 223(d) is unqualified because that section contains no separate reference to obscenity or child pornography. The Government appealed to this Court under the Act's special review provisions, arguing that the District Court erred in holding that the CDA violated both the First Amendment because it is overbroad and the Fifth Amendment because it is vague.

Held: The CDA's "indecent transmission" and "patently offensive display" provisions abridge "the freedom of speech" protected by the First Amendment. Pp. 17–40.

(a) Although the CDA's vagueness is relevant to the First Amendment overbreadth inquiry, the judgment should be affirmed without reaching the Fifth Amendment issue. P. 17.

(b) A close look at the precedents relied on by the Government—*Ginsberg v. New York*, 390 U.S. 629, 20 L. Ed. 2d 195, 88 S. Ct. 1274; *FCC v. Pacifica Foundation*, 438 U.S. 726, 57 L. Ed. 2d 1073, 98 S. Ct. 3026; and *Renton v. Playtime Theatres, Inc.*, 475 U.S. 41, 89 L. Ed. 2d 29, 106 S. Ct. 925—raises, rather than relieves, doubts about the CDA's constitutionality. The CDA differs from the various laws and orders upheld in those cases in many ways, including that it does not allow parents to consent to their children's use of restricted materials; is not limited to commercial transactions; fails to provide any definition of "indecent" and omits any requirement that "patently offensive" material lack socially redeeming value; neither limits its broad categorical prohibitions to particular times nor bases them on an evaluation by an agency familiar with the medium's unique characteristics; is punitive; applies to a medium that, unlike radio, receives full First Amendment protection; and cannot be properly analyzed as a form of time, place, and manner regulation because it is a content-based blanket restriction on speech. These precedents, then, do not require the Court to uphold the CDA and are fully consistent with the application of the most stringent review of its provisions. Pp. 17–21.

(c) The special factors recognized in some of the Court's cases as justifying regulation of the broadcast media—the history of extensive government regulation of broadcasting, see, *e.g., Red Lion Broadcasting Co. v. FCC,* 395 U.S. 367, 399–400, 23 L. Ed. 2d 371, 89 S. Ct. 1794; the scarcity of available frequencies at its inception, see, *e.g., Turner Broadcasting System, Inc. v. FCC,* 512 U.S. 622, 637–638, 129 L. Ed. 2d 497, 114 S. Ct. 2445; and its "invasive" nature, see *Sable Communications of Cal., Inc. v. FCC,* 492 U.S. 115, 128, 106 L. Ed. 2d 93, 109 S. Ct. 2829—are not present in cyberspace. Thus, these cases provide no basis for qualifying the level of First Amendment scrutiny that should be applied to the Internet. Pp. 22–24.

(d) Regardless of whether the CDA is so vague that it violates the Fifth Amendment, the many ambiguities concerning the scope of its coverage render it problematic for First Amendment purposes. For instance, its use of the undefined terms "indecent" and "patently offensive" will provoke uncertainty among speakers about how the two standards relate to each other and just what they mean. The vagueness of such a content-based regulation, see, *e.g., Gentile v. State Bar of Nev.,* 501 U.S. 1030, 115 L. Ed. 2d 888, 111 S. Ct. 2720, coupled with its increased deterrent effect as a criminal statute, see, *e.g., Dombrowski v. Pfister,* 380 U.S. 479, 14 L. Ed. 2d 22, 85 S. Ct. 1116, raise special First Amendment concerns because of its obvious chilling effect on free speech. Contrary to the Government's argument, the CDA is not saved from vagueness by the fact that its "patently offensive" standard repeats the second part of the three-prong obscenity test set forth in *Miller v. California,* 413 U.S. 15, 24, 37 L. Ed. 2d 419, 93 S. Ct. 2607. The second *Miller* prong reduces the inherent vagueness of its own "patently offensive" term by requiring that the proscribed material be "specifically defined by the applicable state law." In addition, *Miller* applies only to "sexual conduct," whereas, the CDA prohibition extends also to "excretory activities" and "organs" of both a sexual and excretory nature. Each of *Miller's* other two prongs also critically limits the uncertain sweep of the obscenity definition. Just because a definition including three limitations is not vague, it does not follow that one of those limitations, standing alone, is not vague. The CDA's vagueness undermines the likelihood that it has been carefully tailored to the congressional goal of protecting minors from potentially harmful materials. Pp. 24–28.

(e) The CDA lacks the precision that the First Amendment requires when a statute regulates the content of speech. Although the Government has an interest in protecting children from potentially harmful materials, see, *e.g.*, *Ginsberg*, 390 U.S. at 639, the CDA pursues that interest by suppressing a large amount of speech that adults have a constitutional right to send and receive, see, *e.g.*, *Sable, supra*, at 126. Its breadth is wholly unprecedented. The CDA's burden on adult speech is unacceptable if less restrictive alternatives would be at least as effective in achieving the Act's legitimate purposes. See, *e.g.*, *Sable*, 492 U.S. at 126. The Government has not proved otherwise. On the other hand, the District Court found that currently available *user-based* software suggests that a reasonably effective method by which *parents* can prevent their children from accessing material which the *parents* believe is inappropriate will soon be widely available. Moreover, the arguments in this Court referred to possible alternatives such as requiring that indecent material be "tagged" to facilitate parental control, making exceptions for messages with artistic or educational value, providing some tolerance for parental choice, and regulating some portions of the Internet differently than others. Particularly in the light of the absence of any detailed congressional findings, or even hearings addressing the CDA's special problems, the Court is persuaded that the CDA is not narrowly tailored. Pp. 28–33.

(f) The Government's three additional arguments for sustaining the CDA's affirmative prohibitions are rejected. First, the contention that the Act is constitutional because it leaves open ample "alternative channels" of communication is unpersuasive because the CDA regulates speech on the basis of its content, so that a "time, place, and manner" analysis is inapplicable. See, *e.g.*, *Consolidated Edison Co. of N.Y. v. Public Serv. Comm'n of N.Y.*, 447 U.S. 530, 536, 65 L. Ed. 2d 319, 100 S. Ct. 2326. Second, the assertion that the CDA's "knowledge" and "specific person" requirements significantly restrict its permissible application to communications to persons the sender knows to be under 18 is untenable, given that most Internet forums are open to all comers and that even the strongest reading of the "specific person" requirement would confer broad powers of censorship, in the form of a "heckler's veto," upon any opponent of indecent speech. Finally, there is no textual support for the submission that material having scientific, educational, or other redeeming social value will necessarily fall outside the CDA's prohibitions. Pp. 33–35.

(g) The § 223(e)(5) defenses do not constitute the sort of "narrow tailoring" that would save the CDA. The Government's argument that transmitters may take protective "good faith action" by "tagging" their indecent communications in a way that would indicate their contents, thus permitting recipients to block their reception with appropriate software, is illusory, given the requirement that such action be "effective": The proposed screening software does not currently exist, but, even if it did, there would be no way of knowing whether a potential recipient would actually block the encoded material. The Government also failed to prove that § 223(b)(5)'s verification defense would significantly reduce the CDA's heavy burden on adult speech. Although such verification is actually being used by some commercial providers of sexually explicit material, the District Court's findings indicate that it is not economically feasible for most noncommercial speakers. Pp. 35–37. . . .

(i) The Government's argument that its "significant" interest in fostering the Internet's growth provides an independent basis for upholding the CDA's constitutionality is singularly unpersuasive. The dramatic expansion of this new forum contradicts the factual basis underlying this contention: that the unregulated availability of "indecent" and "patently offensive" material is driving people away from the Internet. P. 40.

929 F. Supp. 824, *affirmed.*

JUDGES:

Stevens, J., delivered the opinion of the Court, in which Scalia, Kennedy, Souter, Thomas, Ginsburg, and Breyer, JJ., joined. O'Connor, J., filed an opinion concurring in the judgment in part and dissenting in part, in which Rehnquist, C.J., joined.

OPINION:

Justice Stevens delivered the opinion of the Court.

At issue is the constitutionality of two statutory provisions enacted to protect minors from "indecent" and "patently offensive" communications on the Internet. Notwithstanding the legitimacy and importance of the congressional goal of protecting children from harmful materials, we agree with the three-judge District Court that the statute abridges "the freedom of speech" protected by the First Amendment.n1

I

The District Court made extensive findings of fact, most of which were based on a detailed stipulation prepared by the parties. See 929 F. Supp. 824, 830–849 (E.D. Pa. 1996).n2 The findings describe the character and the dimensions of the Internet, the availability of sexually explicit material in that medium, and the problems confronting age verification for recipients of Internet communications. Because those findings provide the underpinnings for the legal issues, we begin with a summary of the undisputed facts.

The Internet

The Internet is an international network of interconnected computers. It is the outgrowth of what began in 1969 as a military program called "ARPANET,"n3 which was designed to enable computers operated by the military, defense contractors, and universities conducting defense-related research to communicate with one another by redundant channels even if some portions of the network were damaged in a war. While the ARPANET no longer exists, it provided an example for the development of a number of civilian networks that, eventually linking with each other, now enable tens of millions of people to communicate with one another and to access vast amounts of information from around the world. The Internet is "a unique and wholly new medium of worldwide human communication."n4

The Internet has experienced "extraordinary growth."n5 The number of "host" computers—those that store information and relay communications—increased from about 300 in 1981 to approximately 9,400,000 by the time of the trial in 1996. Roughly 60% of these hosts are located in the United States. About 40 million people used the Internet at the time of trial, a number that is expected to mushroom to 200 million by 1999.

Individuals can obtain access to the Internet from many different sources, generally hosts themselves or entities with a host affiliation. Most colleges and universities provide access for their students and faculty; many corporations provide their employees with access through an office network; many communities and local libraries provide free access; and an increasing number of storefront "computer coffee shops" provide access for a small hourly fee. Several major national "online services" such as America Online, CompuServe, the Microsoft Network, and Prodigy offer access to their own extensive proprietary networks as well as a link to the much larger resources of the Internet. These commercial online services had almost 12 million individual subscribers at the time of trial.

Anyone with access to the Internet may take advantage of a wide variety of communication and information retrieval methods. These methods are constantly evolving and difficult to categorize precisely. But, as presently constituted, those most relevant to this case are electronic mail ("e-mail"), automatic mailing list services ("mail exploders," sometimes referred to as "listservs"), "newsgroups," "chat rooms," and the "World Wide Web." All of these methods can be used to transmit text; most can transmit sound, pictures, and moving video images. Taken together, these tools constitute a unique medium—known to its users as "cyberspace"—located in no particular geographical location but available to anyone, anywhere in the world, with access to the Internet. . . .

The best known category of communication over the Internet is the World Wide Web, which allows users to search for and retrieve information stored in remote computers, as well as, in some cases, to communicate back to designated sites. . . .

Navigating the Web is relatively straightforward. A user may either type the address of a known page or enter one or more keywords into a commercial "search engine" in an effort to locate sites on a subject of interest. A particular Web page may contain the information sought by the "surfer," or, through its links, it may be an avenue to other documents located anywhere on the Internet. Users generally explore a given Web page, or move to another, by clicking a computer "mouse" on one of the page's icons or links. Access to most Web pages is freely available, but some allow access only to those who have purchased the right from a commercial provider. The Web is thus comparable, from the readers' viewpoint, to both a vast library including millions of readily available and indexed publications and a sprawling mall offering goods and services.

From the publishers' point of view, it constitutes a vast platform from which to address and hear from a world-wide audience of millions of readers, viewers, researchers, and buyers. Any person or organization with a computer connected to the Internet can "publish" information. Publishers include government agencies, educational institutions, commercial entities, advocacy groups, and individuals.[n9] Publishers may either make their material available to the entire pool of Internet users, or confine access to a selected group, such as those willing to pay for the privilege. "No single organization controls any membership in the Web, nor is there any centralized point from which individual Web sites or services can be blocked from the Web."n10

Sexually Explicit Material

Sexually explicit material on the Internet includes text, pictures, and chat and "extends from the modestly titillating to the hardest-core."n11 These files are created, named, and posted in the same manner as material that is not sexually explicit, and may be accessed either deliberately or unintentionally during the course of an imprecise search. "Once a provider posts its content on the Internet, it cannot prevent that content from entering any community."n12 Thus, for example,

> when the UCR/California Museum of Photography posts to its Web site nudes by Edward Weston and Robert Mapplethorpe to announce that its new exhibit will travel to Baltimore and New York City, those images are available not only in Los Angeles, Baltimore, and New York City, but also in Cincinnati, Mobile, or Beijing—wherever Internet users live. Similarly, the safer sex instructions that Critical Path posts to its Web site, written in street language so that the teenage receiver can understand them, are available not just in Philadelphia, but also in Provo and Prague.n13

Some of the communications over the Internet that originate in foreign countries are also sexually explicit.n14

Though such material is widely available, users seldom encounter such content accidentally. "A document's title or a description of the document will usually appear before the document itself . . . and in many cases the user will receive detailed information about a site's content before he or she need take the step to access the document. Almost all sexually explicit images are preceded by warnings as to the content."n15 For that reason, the "odds are slim" that a user would enter a sexually explicit site by accident.n16 Unlike communications received by radio or television, "the receipt of information on the Internet requires a series of affirmative steps more deliberate and directed than merely turning a dial. A child requires some sophistication and some ability to read to retrieve material and thereby to use the Internet unattended."n17

Systems have been developed to help parents control the material that may be available on a home computer with Internet access. A system may either limit a computer's access to an approved list of sources that have been identified as containing no adult material, it may block designated inappropriate sites, or it may attempt to block messages containing identifiable objectionable features. "Although parental control software currently can screen for certain suggestive words or for known sexually explicit sites, it cannot now screen for sexually explicit images."n18 Nevertheless, the evidence indicates that "a reasonably effective method by which parents can prevent their children from accessing sexually explicit and other material which parents may believe is inappropriate for their children will soon be available."n19

Age Verification

The problem of age verification differs for different uses of the Internet. The District Court categorically determined that there "is no effective way to determine the identity or the age of a user who is accessing material through e-mail, mail exploders, newsgroups or chat rooms."n20 The Government offered no evidence that there was a reliable way to screen recipients and participants in such fora for age. Moreover, even if it were technologically feasible to block minors' access to newsgroups and chat rooms containing discussions of art, politics or other subjects that potentially elicit "indecent" or "patently offensive" contributions, it would not be possible to block their access to that material and "still allow them access to the remaining content, even if the overwhelming majority of that content was not indecent."n21

Technology exists by which an operator of a Web site may condition access on the verification of requested information such as a credit card number or an adult password. Credit card verification is only feasible, however, either in connection with a commercial transaction in which the card is used, or by payment to a verification agency. Using credit card possession as a surrogate for proof of age would impose costs on non-commercial Web sites that would require many of them to shut down. For that reason, at the time of the trial, credit card verification was "effectively unavailable to a substantial number of Internet content providers." *Id.*, at 846 (finding 102). Moreover, the imposition of such a requirement "would completely bar adults who do not have a credit card and lack the resources to obtain one from accessing any blocked material."n22

Commercial pornographic sites that charge their users for access have assigned them passwords as a method of age verification. The record does not contain any evidence concerning the reliability of these technologies. Even if passwords are effective for commercial purveyors of indecent material, the District Court found that an adult password requirement would impose significant burdens on noncommercial sites, both because they would discourage users from accessing their sites and because the cost of creating and maintaining such screening systems would be "beyond their reach."n23

In sum, the District Court found:

Even if credit card verification or adult password verification were implemented, the Government presented no testimony as to how such systems could ensure that the user of the password or credit card is in fact over 18. The burdens imposed by credit card verification and adult password verification systems make them effectively unavailable to a substantial number of Internet content providers." *Ibid.* (finding 107).

II

The Telecommunications Act of 1996, Pub. L. 104-104, 110 Stat. 56, was an unusually important legislative enactment. As stated on the first of its 103 pages, its primary purpose was to reduce regulation and encourage "the rapid deployment of new telecommunications technologies." The major components of the statute have nothing to do with the Internet; they were designed to promote competition in the local telephone service market, the multichannel video market, and the market for over-the-air broadcasting. The Act includes seven Titles, six of which are the product of extensive committee hearings and the subject of discussion in Reports prepared by Committees of the Senate and the House of Representatives. By contrast, Title V—known as the "Communications Decency Act of 1996" (CDA)—contains provisions that were either added in executive committee after the hearings were concluded or as amendments offered during floor debate on the legislation. An amendment offered in the Senate was the source of the two statutory provisions challenged in this case.n24 They are informally described as the "indecent transmission" provision and the "patently offensive display" provision.n25

The first, 47 U.S.C.A. § 223(a) (Supp. 1997), prohibits the knowing transmission of obscene or indecent messages to any recipient under 18 years of age. It provides in pertinent part:

(a) Whoever—

    (1) in interstate or foreign communications—

    . . .

      (B) by means of a telecommunications device knowingly—

        (i) makes, creates, or solicits, and

        (ii) initiates the transmission of,

any comment, request, suggestion, proposal, image, or other communication which is obscene or indecent, knowing that the recipient of the communication is under 18 years of age, regardless of whether the maker of such communication placed the call or initiated the communication;

    . . .

    (2) knowingly permits any telecommunications facility under his control to be used for any activity prohibited by paragraph (1) with the intent that it be used for such activity,

    shall be fined under Title 18, or imprisoned not more than two years, or both.

The second provision, § 223(d), prohibits the knowing sending or displaying of patently offensive messages in a manner that is available to a person under 18 years of age. It provides:

(d) Whoever—

    (1) in interstate or foreign communications knowingly—

      (A) uses an interactive computer service to send to a specific person or persons under 18 years of age, or

      (B) uses any interactive computer service to display in a manner available to a person under 18 years of age,

any comment, request, suggestion, proposal, image, or other communication that, in context, depicts or describes, in terms patently offensive as measured by contemporary community standards, sexual or excretory activities or organs, regardless of whether the user of such service placed the call or initiated the communication; or

(2) knowingly permits any telecommunications facility under such person's control to be used for an activity prohibited by paragraph (1) with the intent that it be used for such activity,

shall be fined under Title 18, or imprisoned not more than two years, or both.

The breadth of these prohibitions is qualified by two affirmative defenses. See § 223(e)(5).n26 One covers those who take "good faith, reasonable, effective, and appropriate actions" to restrict access by minors to the prohibited communications. § 223(e)(5)(A). The other covers those who restrict access to covered material by requiring certain designated forms of age proof, such as a verified credit card or an adult identification number or code. § 223(e)(5)(B).

III

On February 8, 1996, immediately after the President signed the statute, 20 plaintiffs n27 filed suit against the Attorney General of the United States and the Department of Justice challenging the constitutionality of §§ 223(a)(1) and 223(d). A week later, based on his conclusion that the term "indecent" was too vague to provide the basis for a criminal prosecution, District Judge Buckwalter entered a temporary restraining order against enforcement of § 223(a)(1)(B)(ii) insofar as it applies to indecent communications. A second suit was then filed by 27 additional plaintiffs,n28 the two cases were consolidated, and a three-judge District Court was convened pursuant to § 561 of the Act.n29 After an evidentiary hearing, that Court entered a preliminary injunction against enforcement of both of the challenged provisions. Each of the three judges wrote a separate opinion, but their judgment was unanimous.

Chief Judge Sloviter doubted the strength of the Government's interest in regulating "the vast range of online material covered or potentially covered by the CDA," but acknowledged that the interest was "compelling" with respect to some of that material. 929 F. Supp. at 853. She concluded, nonetheless, that the statute "sweeps more broadly than necessary and thereby chills the expression of adults" and that the terms "patently offensive" and "indecent" were "inherently vague." *Id.*, at 854. She also determined that the affirmative defenses were not "technologically or economically feasible for most providers," specifically considering and rejecting an argument that providers could avoid liability by "tagging" their material in a manner that would allow potential readers to screen out unwanted transmissions. *Id.*, at 856. Chief Judge Sloviter also rejected the Government's suggestion that the scope of the statute could be narrowed by construing it to apply only to commercial pornographers. *Id.*, at 854–855.

Judge Buckwalter concluded that the word "indecent" in § 223(a)(1)(B) and the terms "patently offensive" and "in context" in § 223(d)(1) were so vague that criminal enforcement of either section would violate the "fundamental constitutional principle" of "simple fairness," *id.*, at 861, and the specific protections of the First and Fifth Amendments, *id.*, at 858. He found no statutory basis for the Government's argument that the challenged provisions would be applied only to "pornographic" materials, noting that, unlike obscenity, "indecency has *not* been defined to exclude works of serious literary, artistic, political or scientific value." *Id.*, at 863. Moreover, the Government's claim that the work must be considered patently offensive "in context" was itself vague because the relevant context might "refer to, among other things, the nature of the communication as a whole, the time of day it was conveyed, the medium used, the identity of the speaker, or whether or not it is accompanied by appropriate warnings." *Id.*, at 864. He believed that the unique nature of the Internet aggravated the vagueness of the statute. *Id.*, at 865, n.9.

Judge Dalzell's review of "the special attributes of Internet communication" disclosed by the evidence convinced him that the First Amendment denies Congress the power to regulate the content of protected speech on the Internet. *Id.*, at 867. His opinion explained at length why he believed the Act would abridge significant protected speech, particularly by noncommercial speakers, while "perversely, commercial pornographers would remain relatively unaffected." *Id.*, at 879. He construed our cases as requiring a "medium-specific" approach to the analysis of the regulation of mass communication, *id.*, at 873, and concluded that the Internet—as "the most participatory form of mass speech yet developed," *id.*, at 883—is entitled to "the highest protection from governmental intrusion." *Ibid.*n30

The judgment of the District Court enjoins the Government from enforcing the prohibitions in § 223(a)(1)(B) insofar as they relate to "indecent" communications, but expressly preserves the Government's right to investigate and prosecute the obscenity or child pornography activities prohibited therein. The injunction against enforcement of §§ 223(d)(1) and (2) is unqualified because those provisions contain no separate reference to obscenity or child pornography.

The Government appealed under the Act's special review provisions, §
561, 110 Stat. 142–143, and we noted probable jurisdiction, see 519 U.S.
(1996). In its appeal, the Government argues that the District Court erred in
holding that the CDA violated both the First Amendment because it is overbroad and the Fifth Amendment because it is vague. While we discuss the
vagueness of the CDA because of its relevance to the First Amendment overbreadth inquiry, we conclude that the judgment should be affirmed without
reaching the Fifth Amendment issue. We begin our analysis by reviewing the
principal authorities on which the Government relies. Then, . . . [we] de-
scrib[e] the overbreadth of the CDA. . . .

IV

In arguing for reversal, the Government contends that the CDA is plainly
constitutional under three of our prior decisions: (1) *Ginsberg v. New York*, 390
U.S. 629, 20 L. Ed. 2d 195, 88 S. Ct. 1274 (1968); (2) *FCC v. Pacifica Foundation*, 438 U.S. 726, 57 L. Ed. 2d 1073, 98 S. Ct. 3026 (1978); and (3) *Renton v.
Playtime Theatres, Inc.*, 475 U.S. 41, 89 L. Ed. 2d 29, 106 S. Ct. 925 (1986). A
close look at these cases, however, raises—rather than relieves—doubts concerning the constitutionality of the CDA.

In *Ginsberg*, we upheld the constitutionality of a New York statute that
prohibited selling to minors under 17 years of age material that was considered obscene as to them even if not obscene as to adults. We rejected the defendant's broad submission that "the scope of the constitutional freedom of
expression secured to a citizen to read or see material concerned with sex cannot be made to depend on whether the citizen is an adult or a minor." 390
U.S. at 636. In rejecting that contention, we relied not only on the State's
independent interest in the well-being of its youth, but also on our consistent
recognition of the principle that "the parents' claim to authority in their
own household to direct the rearing of their children is basic in the structure
of our society."n31 In four important respects, the statute upheld in *Ginsberg*
was narrower than the CDA. First, we noted in *Ginsberg* that "the prohibition
against sales to minors does not bar parents who so desire from purchasing
the magazines for their children." *Id.*, at 639. Under the CDA, by contrast,
neither the parents' consent—nor even their participation—in the communication would avoid the application of the statute.n32 Second, the New
York statute applied only to commercial transactions, *id.*, at 647, whereas the
CDA contains no such limitation. Third, the New York statute cabined its

definition of material that is harmful to minors with the requirement that it be "utterly without redeeming social importance for minors." *Id.*, at 646. The CDA fails to provide us with any definition of the term "indecent" as used in § 223(a)(1) and, importantly, omits any requirement that the "patently offensive" material covered by § 223(d) lack serious literary, artistic, political, or scientific value. Fourth, the New York statute defined a minor as a person under the age of 17, whereas the CDA, in applying to all those under 18 years, includes an additional year of those nearest majority.

In *Pacifica*, we upheld a declaratory order of the Federal Communications Commission, holding that the broadcast of a recording of a 12-minute monologue entitled "Filthy Words" that had previously been delivered to a live audience "could have been the subject of administrative sanctions." 438 U.S. at 730 (internal quotations omitted). The Commission had found that the repetitive use of certain words referring to excretory or sexual activities or organs "in an afternoon broadcast when children are in the audience was patently offensive" and concluded that the monologue was indecent "as broadcast." *Id.*, at 735. The respondent did not quarrel with the finding that the afternoon broadcast was patently offensive, but contended that it was not "indecent" within the meaning of the relevant statutes because it contained no prurient appeal. After rejecting respondent's statutory arguments, we confronted its two constitutional arguments: (1) that the Commission's construction of its authority to ban indecent speech was so broad that its order had to be set aside even if the broadcast at issue was unprotected; and (2) that since the recording was not obscene, the First Amendment forbade any abridgement of the right to broadcast it on the radio.

In the portion of the lead opinion not joined by Justices Powell and Blackmun, the plurality stated that the First Amendment does not prohibit all governmental regulation that depends on the content of speech. *Id.*, at 742–743. Accordingly, the availability of constitutional protection for a vulgar and offensive monologue that was not obscene depended on the context of the broadcast. *Id.*, at 744–748. Relying on the premise that "of all forms of communication" broadcasting had received the most limited First Amendment protection, *id.*, at 748–749, the Court concluded that the ease with which children may obtain access to broadcasts, "coupled with the concerns recognized in *Ginsberg*," justified special treatment of indecent broadcasting. *Id.*, at 749–750.

As with the New York statute at issue in *Ginsberg*, there are significant differences between the order upheld in *Pacifica* and the CDA. First, the order in *Pacifica*, issued by an agency that had been regulating radio stations for decades, targeted a specific broadcast that represented a rather dramatic departure from traditional program content in order to designate when—rather than whether—it would be permissible to air such a program in that particular medium. The CDA's broad categorical prohibitions are not limited to particular times and are not dependent on any evaluation by an agency familiar with the unique characteristics of the Internet. Second, unlike the CDA, the Commission's declaratory order was not punitive; we expressly refused to decide whether the indecent broadcast "would justify a criminal prosecution." *Id.*, at 750. Finally, the Commission's order applied to a medium which as a matter of history had "received the most limited First Amendment protection," *id.*, at 748, in large part because warnings could not adequately protect the listener from unexpected program content. The Internet, however, has no comparable history. Moreover, the District Court found that the risk of encountering indecent material by accident is remote because a series of affirmative steps is required to access specific material.

In *Renton*, we upheld a zoning ordinance that kept adult movie theaters out of residential neighborhoods. The ordinance was aimed, not at the content of the films shown in the theaters, but rather at the "secondary effects"—such as crime and deteriorating property values—that these theaters fostered: " 'It is the secondary effect which these zoning ordinances attempt to avoid, not the dissemination of "offensive" speech.' " 475 U.S. at 49 (quoting *Young v. American Mini Theatres, Inc.*, 427 U.S. 50, 71, n.34, 49 L. Ed. 2d 310, 96 S. Ct. 2440 (1976)). According to the Government, the CDA is constitutional because it constitutes a sort of "cyberzoning" on the Internet. But the CDA applies broadly to the entire universe of cyberspace. And the purpose of the CDA is to protect children from the primary effects of "indecent" and "patently offensive" speech, rather than any "secondary" effect of such speech. Thus, the CDA is a content-based blanket restriction on speech, and, as such, cannot be "properly analyzed as a form of time, place, and manner regulation." 475 U.S. at 46. See also *Boos v. Barry*, 485 U.S. 312, 321, 99 L. Ed. 2d 333, 108 S. Ct. 1157 (1988) ("Regulations that focus on the direct impact of speech on its audience" are not properly analyzed under *Renton*); *Forsyth County v. Nationalist Movement*, 505 U.S. 123, 134, 120 L. Ed. 2d 101, 112 S. Ct. 2395 (1992) ("Listeners' reaction to speech is not a content-neutral basis for regulation").

These precedents, then, surely do not require us to uphold the CDA and are fully consistent with the application of the most stringent review of its provisions.

V

In *Southeastern Promotions, Ltd. v. Conrad*, 420 U.S. 546, 557, 43 L. Ed. 2d 448, 95 S. Ct. 1239 (1975), we observed that "each medium of expression . . . may present its own problems." Thus, some of our cases have recognized special justifications for regulation of the broadcast media that are not applicable to other speakers, see *Red Lion Broadcasting Co. v. FCC*, 395 U.S. 367, 23 L. Ed. 2d 371, 89 S. Ct. 1794 (1969); *FCC v. Pacifica Foundation*, 438 U.S. 726, 57 L. Ed. 2d 1073, 98 S. Ct. 3026 (1978). In these cases, the Court relied on the history of extensive government regulation of the broadcast medium, see, *e.g., Red Lion*, 395 U.S. at 399–400; the scarcity of available frequencies at its inception, see, *e.g., Turner Broadcasting System, Inc. v. FCC*, 512 U.S. 622, 637–638, 129 L. Ed. 2d 497, 114 S. Ct. 2445 (1994); and its "invasive" nature, see *Sable Communications of Cal., Inc. v. FCC*, 492 U.S. 115, 128, 106 L. Ed. 2d 93, 109 S. Ct. 2829 (1989).

Those factors are not present in cyberspace. Neither before nor after the enactment of the CDA have the vast democratic fora of the Internet been subject to the type of government supervision and regulation that has attended the broadcast industry.n33 Moreover, the Internet is not as "invasive" as radio or television. The District Court specifically found that "communications over the Internet do not 'invade' an individual's home or appear on one's computer screen unbidden. Users seldom encounter content 'by accident.' " 929 F. Supp. at 844 (finding 88). It also found that "almost all sexually explicit images are preceded by warnings as to the content," and cited testimony that " 'odds are slim' that a user would come across a sexually explicit sight by accident." *Ibid.*

We distinguished *Pacifica* in *Sable*, 492 U.S. at 128, on just this basis. In *Sable*, a company engaged in the business of offering sexually oriented prerecorded telephone messages (popularly known as "dial-a-porn") challenged the constitutionality of an amendment to the Communications Act that imposed a blanket prohibition on indecent as well as obscene interstate commercial telephone messages. We held that the statute was constitutional insofar as it applied to obscene messages but invalid as applied to indecent messages. In attempting to justify the complete ban and criminalization of indecent commercial telephone messages, the Government relied on *Pacifica*, arguing that the ban was necessary to prevent children from gaining access to such messages. We agreed that "there is a compelling interest in protecting the physical and psychological well-being of minors" which extended to shielding them from indecent messages that are not obscene by adult standards, 492 U.S. at 126, but distinguished our "emphatically narrow holding" in *Pacifica* because it did not involve a complete ban and because it involved a different medium of communication. *Id.*, at 127. We explained that "the dial-it medium requires the listener to take affirmative steps to receive the communication." *Id.*, at 127–128. "Placing a telephone call," we continued, "is not the same as turning on a radio and being taken by surprise by an indecent message." *Id.*, at 128.

Finally, unlike the conditions that prevailed when Congress first authorized regulation of the broadcast spectrum, the Internet can hardly be considered a "scarce" expressive commodity. It provides relatively unlimited, low-cost capacity for communication of all kinds. The Government estimates that "as many as 40 million people use the Internet today, and that figure is expected to grow to 200 million by 1999."n34 This dynamic, multifaceted category of communication includes not only traditional print and news services, but also audio, video, and still images, as well as interactive, real-time dialogue. Through the use of chat rooms, any person with a phone line can become a town crier with a voice that resonates farther than it could from any soapbox. Through the use of Web pages, mail exploders, and newsgroups, the same individual can become a pamphleteer. As the District Court found, "the content on the Internet is as diverse as human thought." 929 F. Supp. at 842 (finding 74). We agree with its conclusion that our cases provide no basis for qualifying the level of First Amendment scrutiny that should be applied to this medium.

VI

Regardless of whether the CDA is so vague that it violates the Fifth Amendment, the many ambiguities concerning the scope of its coverage render it problematic for purposes of the First Amendment. For instance, each of the two parts of the CDA uses a different linguistic form. The first uses the word "indecent," 47 U.S.C.A. § 223(a) (Supp. 1997), while the second speaks of material that "in context, depicts or describes, in terms patently offensive as measured by contemporary community standards, sexual or excretory activities or organs," § 223(d). Given the absence of a definition of either term,n35 this difference in language will provoke uncertainty among speakers about how the two standards relate to each other,n36 and just what they mean.n37 Could a speaker confidently assume that a serious discussion about birth control practices, homosexuality, the First Amendment issues raised by the Appendix to our *Pacifica* opinion, or the consequences of prison rape would not violate the CDA? This uncertainty undermines the likelihood that the CDA has been carefully tailored to the congressional goal of protecting minors from potentially harmful materials.

The vagueness of the CDA is a matter of special concern for two reasons. First, the CDA is a content-based regulation of speech. The vagueness of such a regulation raises special First Amendment concerns because of its obvious chilling effect on free speech. See, *e.g.*, *Gentile v. State Bar of Nev.*, 501 U.S. 1030, 1048–1051, 115 L. Ed. 2d 888, 111 S. Ct. 2720 (1991). Second, the CDA is a criminal statute. In addition to the opprobrium and stigma of a criminal conviction, the CDA threatens violators with penalties including up to two years in prison for each act of violation. The severity of criminal sanctions may well cause speakers to remain silent rather than communicate even arguably unlawful words, ideas, and images. See, *e.g.*, *Dombrowski v. Pfister*, 380 U.S. 479, 494, 14 L. Ed. 2d 22, 85 S. Ct. 1116 (1965). As a practical matter, this increased deterrent effect, coupled with the "risk of discriminatory enforcement" of vague regulations, poses greater First Amendment concerns than those implicated by the civil regulation reviewed in *Denver Area Ed. Telecommunications Consortium, Inc. v. FCC*, 518 U.S. 727 (1996).

The Government argues that the statute is no more vague than the obscenity standard this Court established in *Miller v. California*, 413 U.S. 15, 37 L. Ed. 2d 419, 93 S. Ct. 2607 (1973). But that is not so. In *Miller*, this Court reviewed a criminal conviction against a commercial vendor who mailed brochures containing pictures of sexually explicit activities to individuals who had not requested such materials. *Id.*, at 18. Having struggled for some time to establish a definition of obscenity, we set forth in *Miller* the test for obscenity that controls to this day:

(a) whether the average person, applying contemporary community standards would find that the work, taken as a whole, appeals to the prurient interest; (b) whether the work depicts or describes, in a patently offensive way, sexual conduct specifically defined by the applicable state law; and

(c) whether the work, taken as a whole, lacks serious literary, artistic, political, or scientific value." *Id.*, at 24 [internal quotation marks and citations
omitted].

Because the CDA's "patently offensive" standard (and, we assume *arguendo*,
its synonymous "indecent" standard) is one part of the three-prong *Miller*
test, the Government reasons, it cannot be unconstitutionally vague.

The Government's assertion is incorrect as a matter of fact. The second
prong of the *Miller* test—the purportedly analogous standard—contains a
critical requirement that is omitted from the CDA: that the proscribed material be "specifically defined by the applicable state law." This requirement reduces the vagueness inherent in the open-ended term "patently offensive" as
used in the CDA. Moreover, the *Miller* definition is limited to "sexual conduct," whereas the CDA extends also to include (1) "excretory activities" as
well as (2) "organs" of both a sexual and excretory nature.

The Government's reasoning is also flawed. Just because a definition including three limitations is not vague, it does not follow that one of those limitations, standing by itself, is not vague.n38 Each of *Miller's* additional two
prongs—(1) that, taken as a whole, the material appeal to the "prurient" interest, and (2) that it "lack serious literary, artistic, political, or scientific value"—
critically limits the uncertain sweep of the obscenity definition. The second
requirement is particularly important because, unlike the "patently offensive"
and "prurient interest" criteria, it is not judged by contemporary community
standards. See *Pope v. Illinois*, 481 U.S. 497, 500, 95 L. Ed. 2d 439, 107 S. Ct.
1918 (1987). This "societal value" requirement, absent in the CDA, allows appellate courts to impose some limitations and regularity on the definition by
setting, as a matter of law, a national floor for socially redeeming value. The
Government's contention that courts will be able to give such legal limitations
to the CDA's standards is belied by *Miller's* own rationale for having juries determine whether material is "patently offensive" according to community
standards: that such questions are essentially ones of *fact*.n39

In contrast to *Miller* and our other previous cases, the CDA thus presents
a greater threat of censoring speech that, in fact, falls outside the statute's
scope. Given the vague contours of the coverage of the statute, it unquestionably silences some speakers whose messages would be entitled to constitutional protection. That danger provides further reason for insisting that the
statute not be overly broad. The CDA's burden on protected speech cannot
be justified if it could be avoided by a more carefully drafted statute.

VII

We are persuaded that the CDA lacks the precision that the First Amendment requires when a statute regulates the content of speech. In order to deny minors access to potentially harmful speech, the CDA effectively suppresses a large amount of speech that adults have a constitutional right to receive and to address to one another. That burden on adult speech is unacceptable if less restrictive alternatives would be at least as effective in achieving the legitimate purpose that the statute was enacted to serve.

In evaluating the free speech rights of adults, we have made it perfectly clear that "sexual expression which is indecent but not obscene is protected by the First Amendment." *Sable*, 492 U.S. at 126. See also *Carey v. Population Services Int'l*, 431 U.S. 678, 701, 52 L. Ed. 2d 675, 97 S. Ct. 2010 (1977) ("Where obscenity is not involved, we have consistently held that the fact that protected speech may be offensive to some does not justify its suppression"). Indeed, *Pacifica* itself admonished that "the fact that society may find speech offensive is not a sufficient reason for suppressing it." 438 U.S. at 745.

It is true that we have repeatedly recognized the governmental interest in protecting children from harmful materials. See *Ginsberg*, 390 U.S. at 639; *Pacifica*, 438 U.S. at 749. But that interest does not justify an unnecessarily broad suppression of speech addressed to adults. As we have explained, the Government may not "reduce the adult population . . . to . . . only what is fit for children." *Denver*, 518 U.S. at ___ (slip op., at 29) (internal quotation marks omitted) (quoting *Sable*, 492 U.S. at 128).n40 "Regardless of the strength of the government's interest" in protecting children, "the level of discourse reaching a mailbox simply cannot be limited to that which would be suitable for a sandbox." *Bolger v. Youngs Drug Products Corp.*, 463 U.S. 60, 74–75, 77 L. Ed. 2d 469, 103 S. Ct. 2875 (1983).

The District Court was correct to conclude that the CDA effectively resembles the ban on "dial-a-porn" invalidated in *Sable*. 929 F. Supp. 824, 854. In *Sable*, 492 U.S. at 129, this Court rejected the argument that we should defer to the congressional judgment that nothing less than a total ban would be effective in preventing enterprising youngsters from gaining access to indecent communications. *Sable* thus made clear that the mere fact that a statutory regulation of speech was enacted for the important purpose of protecting children from exposure to sexually explicit material does not foreclose inquiry into its validity.n41 As we pointed out last Term, that inquiry embodies an "over-arching commitment" to make sure that Congress has designed its statute to accomplish its purpose "without imposing an unnecessarily great restriction on speech." *Denver*, 518 U.S. at ___ (slip op., at 11).

In arguing that the CDA does not so diminish adult communication, the Government relies on the incorrect factual premise that prohibiting a transmission whenever it is known that one of its recipients is a minor would not interfere with adult-to-adult communication. The findings of the District Court make clear that this premise is untenable. Given the size of the potential audience for most messages, in the absence of a viable age verification process, the sender must be charged with knowing that one or more minors will likely view it. Knowledge that, for instance, one or more members of a 100-person chat group will be minor—and therefore that it would be a crime to send the group an indecent message—would surely burden communication among adults.n42

The District Court found that at the time of trial existing technology did not include any effective method for a sender to prevent minors from obtaining access to its communications on the Internet without also denying access to adults. The Court found no effective way to determine the age of a user who is accessing material through e-mail, mail exploders, newsgroups, or chat rooms. 929 F. Supp. at 845 (findings 90–94). As a practical matter, the Court also found that it would be prohibitively expensive for noncommercial—as well as some commercial—speakers who have Web sites to verify that their users are adults. *Id.*, at 845–848 (findings 95–116).n43 These limitations must inevitably curtail a significant amount of adult communication on the Internet. By contrast, the District Court found that "despite its limitations, currently available *user-based* software suggests that a reasonably effective method by which *parents* can prevent their children from accessing sexually explicit and other material which *parents* may believe is inappropriate for their children will soon be widely available." *Id.*, at 842 (finding 73) (emphases added).

The breadth of the CDA's coverage is wholly unprecedented. Unlike the regulations upheld in *Ginsberg* and *Pacifica*, the scope of the CDA is not limited to commercial speech or commercial entities. Its open-ended prohibitions embrace all nonprofit entities and individuals posting indecent messages or displaying them on their own computers in the presence of minors. The general, undefined terms "indecent" and "patently offensive" cover large amounts of nonpornographic material with serious educational or other value.n44 Moreover, the "community standards" criterion as applied to the Internet means that any communication available to a nation-wide audience will be judged by the standards of the community most likely to be offended by the message.n45 The regulated subject matter includes any of the seven "dirty words" used in the *Pacifica* monologue, the use of which the Government's expert acknowledged could constitute a felony. See Olsen Test., Tr. Vol. V, 53:16–54:10. It may also extend to discussions about prison rape or safe sexual practices, artistic images that include nude subjects, and arguably the card catalogue of the Carnegie Library.

For the purposes of our decision, we need neither accept nor reject the Government's submission that the First Amendment does not forbid a blanket prohibition on all "indecent" and "patently offensive" messages communicated to a 17-year-old—no matter how much value the message may contain and regardless of parental approval. It is at least clear that the strength of the Government's interest in protecting minors is not equally strong throughout the coverage of this broad statute. Under the CDA, a parent allowing her 17-year-old to use the family computer to obtain information on the Internet that she, in her parental judgment, deems appropriate could face a lengthy prison term. See 47 U.S.C.A. § 223(a)(2) (Supp. 1997). Similarly, a parent who sent his 17-year-old college freshman information on birth control via e-mail could be incarcerated even though neither he, his child, nor anyone in their home community, found the material "indecent" or "patently offensive," if the college town's community thought otherwise.

The breadth of this content-based restriction of speech imposes an especially heavy burden on the Government to explain why a less restrictive provision would not be as effective as the CDA. It has not done so. The arguments in this Court have referred to possible alternatives such as requiring that indecent material be "tagged" in a way that facilitates parental control of material coming into their homes, making exceptions for messages with artistic or educational value, providing some tolerance for parental choice, and regulating some portions of the Internet—such as commercial Web sites—differently than others, such as chat rooms. Particularly in the light of the absence of any detailed findings by the Congress, or even hearings addressing the special problems of the CDA, we are persuaded that the CDA is not narrowly tailored if that requirement has any meaning at all.

VIII

In an attempt to curtail the CDA's facial overbreadth, the Government advances three additional arguments for sustaining the Act's affirmative prohibitions: (1) that the CDA is constitutional because it leaves open ample "alternative channels" of communication; (2) that the plain meaning of the

Act's "knowledge" and "specific person" requirement significantly restricts its permissible applications; and (3) that the Act's prohibitions are "almost always" limited to material lacking redeeming social value.

The Government first contends that, even though the CDA effectively censors discourse on many of the Internet's modalities—such as chat groups, newsgroups, and mail exploders—it is nonetheless constitutional because it provides a "reasonable opportunity" for speakers to engage in the restricted speech on the World Wide Web. Brief for Appellants 39. This argument is unpersuasive because the CDA regulates speech on the basis of its content. A "time, place, and manner" analysis is therefore inapplicable. See *Consolidated Edison Co. of N.Y. v. Public Serv. Comm'n of N.Y.*, 447 U.S. 530, 536, 65 L. Ed. 2d 319, 100 S. Ct. 2326 (1980). It is thus immaterial whether such speech would be feasible on the Web (which, as the Government's own expert acknowledged, would cost up to $10,000 if the speaker's interests were not accommodated by an existing Web site, not including costs for database management and age verification). The Government's position is equivalent to arguing that a statute could ban leaflets on certain subjects as long as individuals are free to publish books. In invalidating a number of laws that banned leafletting on the streets *regardless of* their content—we explained that "one is not to have the exercise of his liberty of expression in appropriate places abridged on the plea that it may be exercised in some other place." *Schneider v. State (Town of Irvington)*, 308 U.S. 147, 163, 84 L. Ed. 155, 60 S. Ct. 146 (1939).

The Government also asserts that the "knowledge" requirement of both §§ 223(a) and (d), especially when coupled with the "specific child" element found in § 223(d), saves the CDA from overbreadth. Because both sections prohibit the dissemination of indecent messages only to persons known to be under 18, the Government argues, it does not require transmitters to "refrain from communicating indecent material to adults; they need only refrain from disseminating such materials to persons they know to be under 18." Brief for Appellants 24. This argument ignores the fact that most Internet fora—including chat rooms, newsgroups, mail exploders, and the Web—are open to all comers. The Government's assertion that the knowledge requirement somehow protects the communications of adults is therefore untenable. Even the strongest reading of the "specific person" requirement of § 223(d) cannot save the statute. It would confer broad powers of censorship, in the form of a "heckler's veto," upon any opponent of indecent speech who might simply log on and inform the would-be discoursers that his 17-year-old child—a "specific person . . . under 18 years of age," 47 U.S.C.A. § 223(d)(1)(A) (Supp. 1997)—would be present.

Finally, we find no textual support for the Government's submission that material having scientific, educational, or other redeeming social value will necessarily fall outside the CDA's "patently offensive" and "indecent" prohibitions. See also n.37, *supra*.

IX

The Government's three remaining arguments focus on the defenses provided in § 223(e)(5).n46 First, relying on the "good faith, reasonable, effective, and appropriate actions" provision, the Government suggests that "tagging" provides a defense that saves the constitutionality of the Act. The suggestion assumes that transmitters may encode their indecent communications in a way that would indicate their contents, thus permitting recipients to block their reception with appropriate software. It is the requirement that the good faith action must be "effective" that makes this defense illusory. The Government recognizes that its proposed screening software does not currently exist. Even if it did, there is no way to know whether a potential recipient will actually block the encoded material. Without the impossible knowledge that every guardian in America is screening for the "tag," the transmitter could not reasonably rely on its action to be "effective."

For its second and third arguments concerning defenses—which we can consider together—the Government relies on the latter half of § 223(e)(5), which applies when the transmitter has restricted access by requiring use of a verified credit card or adult identification. Such verification is not only technologically available but actually is used by commercial providers of sexually explicit material. These providers, therefore, would be protected by the defense. Under the findings of the District Court, however, it is not economically feasible for most noncommercial speakers to employ such verification. Accordingly, this defense would not significantly narrow the statute's burden on noncommercial speech. Even with respect to the commercial pornographers that would be protected by the defense, the Government failed to adduce any evidence that these verification techniques actually preclude minors from posing as adults.n47 Given that the risk of criminal sanctions "hovers over each content provider, like the proverbial sword of Damocles,"n48 the District Court correctly refused to rely on unproven future technology to save the statute. The Government thus failed to prove that the proffered defense would significantly reduce the heavy burden on adult speech produced by the prohibition on offensive displays.

We agree with the District Court's conclusion that the CDA places an unacceptably heavy burden on protected speech, and that the defenses do not constitute the sort of "narrow tailoring" that will save an otherwise patently invalid unconstitutional provision. In *Sable*, 492 U.S. at 127, we remarked that the speech restriction at issue there amounted to " 'burning the house to roast the pig.' " The CDA, casting a far darker shadow over free speech, threatens to torch a large segment of the Internet community. . . .

XI

In this Court, though not in the District Court, the Government asserts that—in addition to its interest in protecting children—its "equally significant" interest in fostering the growth of the Internet provides an independent basis for upholding the constitutionality of the CDA. Brief for Appellants 19. The Government apparently assumes that the unregulated availability of "indecent" and "patently offensive" material on the Internet is driving countless citizens away from the medium because of the risk of exposing themselves or their children to harmful material.

We find this argument singularly unpersuasive. The dramatic expansion of this new marketplace of ideas contradicts the factual basis of this contention. The record demonstrates that the growth of the Internet has been and continues to be phenomenal. As a matter of constitutional tradition, in the absence of evidence to the contrary, we presume that governmental regulation of the content of speech is more likely to interfere with the free exchange of ideas than to encourage it. The interest in encouraging freedom of expression in a democratic society outweighs any theoretical but unproven benefit of censorship.

For the foregoing reasons, the judgment of the district court is affirmed. *It is so ordered.*

The opinion of Justice O'Connor, with whom the Chief Justice joins, concurring in the judgment in part and dissenting in part, is omitted.

AMERICAN CIVIL LIBERTIES UNION ET AL. V. RENO IV

No. 99-1324

UNITED STATES COURT OF APPEALS
FOR THE THIRD CIRCUIT

217 F.3d 162; 2000 U.S. App. LEXIS 14419

November 4, 1999, Argued

June 22, 2000, Filed

PRIOR HISTORY:
On Appeal from the United States District Court for the Eastern District of Pennsylvania. (D.C. No. 98-cv-05591). District Judge: Honorable Lowell A. Reed, Jr.

DISPOSITION:
Affirmed.

JUDGES:
Before: Nygaard, McKee, Circuit Judges, and Garth, Senior Circuit Judge.

OPINION OF THE COURT

GARTH, CIRCUIT JUDGE:
This appeal "presents a conflict between one of society's most cherished rights—freedom of expression—and one of the government's most profound obligations—the protection of minors." *American Booksellers v. Webb*, 919 F.2d

1493, 1495 (11th Cir. 1990). The Government challenges the District Court's issuance of a preliminary injunction which prevents the enforcement of the Child Online Protection Act, Pub. L. No. 105–277, 112 Stat. 2681 (1998) (codified at 47 U.S.C. § 231) ("COPA"), enacted in October of 1998. At issue is COPA's constitutionality, a statute designed to protect minors from "harmful material" measured by "contemporary community standards" knowingly posted on the World Wide Web ("Web") for commercial purposes [footnote omitted].

We will affirm the District Court's grant of a preliminary injunction because we are confident that the ACLU's attack on COPA's constitutionality is likely to succeed on the merits. Because material posted on the Web is accessible by all Internet users worldwide, and because current technology does not permit a Web publisher to restrict access to its site based on the geographic locale of each particular Internet user, COPA essentially requires that every Web publisher subject to the statute abide by the most restrictive and conservative state's community standards in order to avoid criminal liability. Thus, because the standard by which COPA gauges whether material is "harmful to minors" is based on identifying "contemporary community standards," the inability of Web publishers to restrict access to their Web sites based on the geographic locale of the site visitor, in and of itself, imposes an impermissible burden on constitutionally protected First Amendment speech.

In affirming the District Court, we are forced to recognize that, at present, due to technological limitations, there may be no other means by which harmful material on the Web may be constitutionally restricted, although, in light of rapidly developing technological advances, what may now be impossible to regulate constitutionally may, in the not-too-distant future, become feasible.

I. Background

COPA was enacted into law on October 21, 1998. Commercial Web publishers subject to the statute that distribute material that is harmful to minors are required under COPA to ensure that minors do not access the harmful material on their Web site. COPA is Congress' second attempt to regulate the dissemination to minors of indecent material on the Web/Internet. The Supreme Court had earlier, on First Amendment grounds, struck down Congress' first endeavor, the Communications Decency Act ("CDA"), which it passed as part of the Telecommunications Act of 1996.n2 See *ACLU v. Reno,*

521 U.S. 844, 138 L. Ed. 2d 874, 117 S. Ct. 2329 (1997) *(Reno II)*. To best understand the current challenge to COPA, it is necessary for us to briefly examine the CDA.

A. CDA

The CDA prohibited Internet users from using the Internet to communicate material that, under contemporary community standards, would be deemed patently offensive to minors under the age of eighteen. See *Reno II*, 521 U.S. at 859–60 (footnote omitted). In so restricting Internet users, the CDA provided two affirmative defenses to prosecution: (1) the use of a credit card or other age verification system, and (2) any good faith effort to restrict access by minors. See *id.*, at 860. In holding that the CDA violated the First Amendment, the Supreme Court explained that without defining key terms the statute was unconstitutionally vague. Moreover, the Court noted that the breadth of the CDA was "wholly unprecedented" in that, for example, it was "not limited to commercial speech or commercial entities . . . [but rather] its open-ended prohibitions embrace all nonprofit entities and individuals posting indecent messages or displaying them on their own computers." *Id.* at 877.

Further, the Court explained that, as applied to the Internet, a community standards criterion would effectively mean that because all Internet communication is made available to a worldwide audience, the content of the conveyed message will be judged by the standards of the community most likely to be offended by the content. See *id.* at 877–78. Finally, with respect to the affirmative defenses authorized by the CDA, the Court concluded that such defenses would not be economically feasible for most noncommercial Web publishers, and that even with respect to commercial publishers, the technology had yet to be proven effective in shielding minors from harmful material. See *id.* at 881. As a result, the Court held that the CDA was not tailored so narrowly as to achieve the government's compelling interest in protecting minors, and that it lacked the precision that the First Amendment requires when a statute regulates the content of speech. See *id.*, at 874. See also *United States v. Playboy Entertainment Group, Inc.*, 529 U.S. 803, 146 L. Ed. 2d 865, 120 S. Ct. 1878, 2000 WL 646196 (U.S. 2000).

B. COPA

COPA, the present statute, attempts to "address[ ] the specific concerns raised by the Supreme Court" in invalidating the CDA. H.R. Rep. No. 105-775, at

12 (1998); see S.R. Rep. No. 105-225, at 2 (1998). COPA prohibits an individual or entity from:

> knowingly and with knowledge of the character of the material, in interstate or foreign commerce by means of the World Wide Web, making any communication for commercial purposes that is available to any minor and that includes any material that is harmful to minors. 47 U.S.C. § 231(a)(1) (emphasis added).

As part of its attempt to cure the constitutional defects found in the CDA, Congress sought to define most of COPA's key terms. COPA attempts, for example, to restrict its scope to material on the Web rather than on the Internet as a whole;n4 to target only those Web communications made for "commercial purposes";n5 and to limit its scope to only that material deemed "harmful to minors."

Under COPA, whether material published on the Web is "harmful to minors" is governed by a three-part test, each of which must be found before liability can attach:n6

> (A) the average person, applying contemporary community standards, would find, taking the material as a whole and with respect to minors, is designed to appeal to, or is designed to pander to, the prurient interest;

> (B) depicts, describes, or represents, in a manner patently offensive with respect to minors, an actual or simulated sexual act or sexual contact, an actual or simulated normal or perverted sexual act, or a lewd exhibition of the genitals or post-pubescent female breast; and

> (C) taken as a whole, lacks serious, literary, artistic, political, or scientific value for minors. 47 U.S.C. § 231(e)(6) (emphasis added).n7

The parties conceded at oral argument that this "contemporary community standards" test applies to those communities within the United States, and not to foreign communities. Therefore, the more liberal community standards of Amsterdam or the more restrictive community standards of Tehran would not impact upon the analysis of whether material is "harmful to minors" under COPA.

COPA also provides Web publishers subject to the statute with affirmative defenses. If a Web publisher "has restricted access by minors to material that is harmful to minors" through the use of a "credit card, debit account, adult access code, or adult personal identification number . . . a digital certificate that verifies age . . . or by any other reasonable measures that are feasible under available technology," then no liability will attach to the Web publisher even if a minor should nevertheless gain access to restricted material under COPA. 47 U.S.C. § 231(c)(1).n8 COPA violators face both criminal (maximum fines of $50,000 and a maximum prison term of six months, or both) and civil (fines of up to $50,000 for each day of violation) penalties.n9

C. Overview of the Internet and the World Wide Web

In recent years use of the Internet and the Web has become increasingly common in mainstream society. . . .

It is essential to note that under current technology, Web publishers cannot "prevent [their site's] content from entering any geographic community." *Reno III*, 31 F. Supp. 2d at 484. As such, Web publishers cannot prevent Internet users in certain geographic locales from accessing their site; and in fact the Web publisher will not even know the geographic location of visitors to its site. See *American Libraries*, 969 F. Supp. at 171. Similarly, a Web publisher cannot modify the content of its site so as to restrict different geographic communities to access of only certain portions of their site. Thus, once published on the Web, existing technology does not permit the published material to be restricted to particular states or jurisdictions.

D. Procedural History

On October 22, 1998, the day after COPA was enacted, the American Civil Liberties Union ("ACLU") brought the present action in the United States District Court for the Eastern District of Pennsylvania, challenging COPA's constitutionality and seeking to enjoin its enforcement.n13 After granting a temporary restraining order against enforcement of the law on November 20, 1998, the District Court held extensive evidentiary hearings which, on February 1, 1999, resulted in the entry of a preliminary injunction preventing the government from enforcing COPA.

E. District Court's Findings of Fact

After five days of testimony, the District Court rendered sixty-seven separate findings of fact concerning the Internet, the Web, and COPA's impact on speech activity in this relatively-new medium. See *Reno III*, 31 F. Supp. 2d at 482–92. It bears noting that none of the parties dispute the District Court's findings (including those describing the Internet and the Web), nor are any challenged as clearly erroneous. Thus, we accept these findings.

The District Court first rendered findings concerning the physical medium known as the Internet, which it recognized consisted of many different methods of communication, only one of which is the World Wide Web. See *Reno III*, 31 F. Supp. 2d at 482–83. It found that "once a provider posts its content on the Internet and chooses to make it available to all, it generally cannot prevent that content from entering any geographical community." *Id.*

The Court then made findings as to the costs and burdens COPA imposes on Web publishers and on the adults who seek access to sites covered by COPA. See *Reno III*, 31 F. Supp. 2d at 482–92. As observed earlier, the statute provides for a limited number of defenses for Web publishers. See 47 U.S.C. § 231(c).n14 The Court found that as a technological matter the only affirmative defenses presently available are the implementation of credit card or age verification systems because there is no currently functional digital certificate or other reasonable means to verify age. See *Reno III*, 31 F. Supp. 2d at 487.

With respect to the credit card option, the court found that the cost to Web publishers could range from $300 to "thousands of dollars" (exclusive of transaction fees incurred from each verification). *Id.* at 488. These costs were also exclusive, according to the court, of the labor and energy that would be required of the Web publisher to implement such a system. *Id.* This labor and energy would include reorganizing a particular Web site to ensure that material considered "harmful to minors" could only be accessed after passing through a credit card or other age verification system. See *id.* at 490. With this in mind, the court found, for example, that textual material that consisted primarily of non-sexual material, but also included some content that was "harmful to minors" would also be subject to such age verification systems. See *id.*

As for age verification systems, the District Court's findings were more optimistic. The court found that a Web publisher "can sign up for free with Adult Check [one company providing such a service] to accept Adult Check PINs, and a Web site operator can earn commissions of up to 50% to 60% of the fees generated by [their] users." *Id.* at 489. The District Court also downplayed the cost (both in price and in energy) that would be incurred by the individual seeking to access "harmful to minors" material on the Web, finding that an Adult Check password could be easily purchased for only $16.95. See *id.* at 490.n15 The same burdens concerning the reorganization of a particular Web site mentioned above would, of course, equally apply to a Web publisher that elected to utilize a PIN number for age verification.

Either system, according to the District Court, would impose significant residual or indirect burdens upon Web publishers. Most importantly, both credit card and age verification systems require an individual seeking to access material otherwise permissible to adults to reveal personal statistics. Because many adults will choose not to reveal these personal details, those otherwise frequently visited Web sites will experience "a loss of traffic." *Id.* at 491. This loss of traffic, in turn, would inflict "economic harm" upon the particular Web site, thus increasing the burden that COPA imposes. *Id.* at P 61.

Finally, the District Court considered whether voluntary parental blocking or filtering software was a less restrictive means by which to achieve the government's compelling objective of protecting minors from harmful material on the Web. The court found that "such technology may be downloaded and installed on a user's home computer at a price of approximately $ 40.00." 31 F. Supp. 2d at 492 P 65. The court, however, acknowledged that such software "is not perfect" as it is both over and under inclusive in the breadth of the material that it blocks and filters. See *id.* P 66.n16

F. District Court's Conclusions of Law

Initially, the government moved the District Court to dismiss the ACLU's action insofar as the individuals and entities that it purported to represent were not in danger of prosecution under COPA and therefore lacked standing. In particular, the government asserted that the material placed on plaintiffs' Web sites was not "harmful to minors" and that each of the plaintiffs were not "engaged in the business" of posting such material for "commercial purposes." See *supra* note 13.

The District Court interpreted COPA to impose liability on those Web publishers who profited from Web sites that contained some, even though not all, material that was harmful to minors. See *Reno III*, 31 F. Supp. 2d at 480. The court therefore concluded that the plaintiffs could reasonably fear prosecution because their Web sites contained material "that is sexual in nature." *Id.*

Having established plaintiffs' standing n17—an analysis with which we agree—the District Court began its First Amendment analysis by stating that insofar as COPA prohibits Web publishers from posting material that is "harmful to minors," it constitutes a content-based restriction on speech that "is presumptively invalid and is subject to strict scrutiny." *Id.* at 493 (citing *R.A.V. v. City of St. Paul*, 505 U.S. 377, 381, 120 L. Ed. 2d 305, 112 S. Ct. 2538 (1992); *Sable Comm. of Calif. v. FCC*, 492 U.S. 115, 126, 106 L. Ed. 2d 93, 109 S. Ct. 2829 (1989)). See also *United States v. Playboy Entertainment Group, Inc.*, 529 U.S. 803, 120 S. Ct. 1878, 146 L. Ed. 2d 865, 2000 WL 646196 (U.S. 2000). Pursuant to this strict scrutiny analysis, the District Court held that COPA placed too large a burden on protected expression. In particular, the court found that the high economic costs that Web publishers would incur in implementing an age verification system would cause them to cease publishing such material, and further, that the difficulty in accurately shielding harmful material from minors would lead Web publishers to censor more material than necessary. See *id.* at 494–95. Moreover, the District Court believed that because of the need to use age verification systems, adults would be deterred from accessing these sites, and that the resulting loss of Web traffic would affect the Web publishers' abilities to continue providing such communications in the future.

The court then considered whether the government could establish that COPA was the least restrictive and most narrowly tailored means to achieve its compelling objective. See *Reno III*, 31 F. Supp. 2d at 496. The government contends that COPA meets this test because COPA does not " 'ban . . . the distribution or display of material harmful to minors [but] simply requires the sellers of such material to recast their message so that they are not readily available to children.' " Appellant's Brief at 27 (quoting H.R. Rep. No. 105-775 at 6 (1998)). The court concluded, however, that even if COPA were enforced, children would still be able to access numerous foreign Web sites containing harmful material; that some minors legitimately possess credit cards—thus defeating the effectiveness of this affirmative defense in restricting access by minors; that COPA prohibits a "sweeping category of form of content" instead of limiting its coverage to pictures, images and graphic image files—most often utilized by the adult industry as "teasers" *Reno III*, 31 F. Supp. 2d at 497; and that parental blocking and filtering technology would likely be as effective as COPA while imposing fewer constitutional burdens on free speech. Therefore, the District Court concluded that COPA was not the least restrictive means for the government to achieve its compelling objective of protecting minors from harmful material. *Id.* at 492. As a result, the court held that the ACLU had shown a substantial likelihood of succeeding on the merits in establishing COPA's unconstitutionality.

In concluding its analysis, the District Court held that losing First Amendment freedoms, even if only for a moment, constitutes irreparable harm. See *id.* (citing *Hohe v. Casey*, 868 F.2d 69, 72–73 (3d Cir. 1989)). And, in balancing the interests at stake for issuing a preliminary injunction, the District Court concluded that the scale tipped in favor of the ACLU, as the government lacks an interest in enforcing an unconstitutional law. See *id.* (citing *ACLU v. Reno*, 929 F. Supp. 824, 849 (E.D. Pa. 1996)). Because the ACLU met its burden for a preliminary injunction, the District Court granted its petition.

II. Analysis

In determining whether a preliminary injunction is warranted, we must consider: (1) whether the movant has shown a reasonable probability of success on the merits; (2) whether the movant will be irreparably harmed by denial of the relief; (3) whether granting preliminary relief will result in even greater harm to the nonmoving party; and (4) whether granting the preliminary relief will be in the public interest. *Allegheny Energy, Inc. v. DQE, Inc.*, 171 F.3d 153, 158 (3d Cir. 1999) (citing *ACLU v. Black Horse Pike Regional Bd. of Educ.*, 84 F.3d 1471, 1477 n.2 (3d Cir. 1996) (en banc)).

We review a district court's grant of a preliminary injunction according to a three-part standard. Legal conclusions are reviewed de novo, findings of fact are reviewed for clear error, and the "ultimate decision to grant or deny the preliminary injunction" is reviewed for abuse of discretion. See *Maldonado v. Houstoun*, 157 F.3d 179, 183 (3d Cir. 1998), cert. denied, 526 U.S. 1130, 119 S. Ct. 1802, 143 L. Ed. 2d 1007 (1999).

A. Reasonable Probability of Success on the Merits

We begin our analysis by considering what, for this case, is the most significant prong of the preliminary injunction test—whether the ACLU met its burden of establishing a reasonable probability of succeeding on the merits in proving that COPA trenches upon the First Amendment to the United States Constitution. Initially, we note that the District Court correctly determined that as a content-based restriction on speech, COPA is "both presumptively invalid and subject to strict scrutiny analysis." See *Reno III*, 31 F. Supp. 2d at

493. As in all areas of constitutional strict scrutiny jurisprudence, the government must establish that the challenged statute is narrowly tailored to meet a compelling state interest, and that it seeks to protect its interest in a manner that is the least restrictive of protected speech. See, *e.g.*, *Schaumberg v. Citizens for a Better Environment*, 444 U.S. 620, 637, 63 L. Ed. 2d 73, 100 S. Ct. 826 (1980); *Sable Comm. of Calif. v. FCC*, 492 U.S. 115, 126, 106 L. Ed. 2d 93, 109 S. Ct. 2829 (1989).n18 These principles have been emphasized again in the Supreme Court's most recent opinion, *United States v. Playboy Entertainment Group, Inc.*, 529 U.S. 803, 120 S. Ct. 1878, 146 L. Ed. 2d 865, 2000 WL 646196 (U.S. 2000), where the Court, concerned with the "bleeding" of cable transmissions, held § 505 of the Telecommunications Act of 1996 unconstitutional as violative of the First Amendment.

It is undisputed that the government has a compelling interest in protecting children from material that is harmful to them, even if not obscene by adult standards. See *Reno III*, 31 F. Supp. 2d at 495 (citing *Sable*, 492 U.S. at 126 (1989); *Ginsberg v. New York*, 390 U.S. 629, 639–40, 20 L. Ed. 2d 195, 88 S. Ct. 1274 (1968)). At issue is whether, in achieving this compelling objective, Congress has articulated a constitutionally permissible means to achieve its objective without curtailing the protected free speech rights of adults. See *Reno III*, 31 F. Supp. 2d at 492 (citing *Sable*, 492 U.S. at 127; *Butler v. Michigan*, 352 U.S. 380, 383, 1 L. Ed. 2d 412, 77 S. Ct. 524 (1957)). As we have observed, the District Court found that it had not—holding that COPA was not likely to succeed in surviving strict scrutiny analysis.

We base our particular determination of COPA's likely unconstitutionality, however, on COPA's reliance on "contemporary community standards" in the context of the electronic medium of the Web to identify material that is harmful to minors. The overbreadth of COPA's definition of "harmful to minors" applying a "contemporary community standards" clause—although virtually ignored by the parties and the amicus in their respective briefs but raised by us at oral argument—so concerns us that we are persuaded that this aspect of COPA, without reference to its other provisions, must lead inexorably to a holding of a likelihood of unconstitutionality of the entire COPA statute. Hence we base our opinion entirely on the basis of the likely unconstitutionality of this clause, even though the District Court relied on numerous other grounds.n19

As previously noted, in passing COPA, Congress attempted to resolve all of the problems raised by the Supreme Court in striking down the CDA as unconstitutional. One concern noted by the Supreme Court was that, as a part of the wholly unprecedented broad coverage of the CDA, "the 'community standards' criterion as applied to the Internet means that any communication available to a nationwide audience will be judged by the standards of the community most likely to be offended by the message." *Reno II*, 521 U.S. at 877–78. We are not persuaded that the Supreme Court's concern with respect to the "community standards" criterion has been sufficiently remedied by Congress in COPA.

Previously, in addressing the mailing of unsolicited sexually explicit material in violation of a California obscenity statute, the Supreme Court held that the fact-finder must determine whether " 'the average person, applying contemporary community standards,' would find the work taken as a whole, [to appeal] to the prurient interest." *Miller v. California*, 413 U.S. 15, 24, 37 L. Ed. 2d 419, 93 S. Ct. 2607 (1973) (quoting *Kois v. Wisconsin*, 408 U.S. 229, 230, 33 L. Ed. 2d 312, 92 S. Ct. 2245 (1972)). In response to the Supreme Court's criticism of the CDA, Congress incorporated into COPA this *Miller* test, explaining that in so doing COPA now "conforms to the standards identified in *Ginsberg*, as modified by the Supreme Court in *Miller v. California*, 413 U.S. 15, 37 L. Ed. 2d 419, 93 S. Ct. 2607 (1973)." H.R. Rep. No. 105-775 at 13 (1998); 47 U.S.C. § 231(e)(6)(A). Even in so doing, Congress remained cognizant of the fact that "the application of community standards in the context of the Web is controversial." H.R. Rep. No. 107-775, at 28. Nevertheless, in defending the constitutionality of COPA's use of the *Miller* test, the government insists that "there is nothing dispositive about the fact that [in COPA] commercial distribution of such [harmful] materials occurs through an online, rather than a brick and mortar outlet." See Reply Brief at 18 n.3.

Despite the government's assertion, "each medium of expression 'must be assessed for First Amendment purposes by standards suited to it, for each may present its own problems.' " *Reno III*, 31 F. Supp. 2d at 495 (quoting *Southeastern Promotions, Ltd v. Conrad*, 420 U.S. 546, 557, 43 L. Ed. 2d 448, 95 S. Ct. 1239 (1975)). See also *United States v. Playboy Entertainment Group, Inc.*, 529 U.S. 803, 120 S. Ct. 1878, 146 L. Ed. 2d 865, 2000 WL 646196, at *8 (U.S. 2000). In considering "the unique factors that affect communication in the new and technology-laden medium of the Web," we are convinced that there are crucial differences between a "brick and mortar outlet" and the online Web that dramatically affect a First Amendment analysis. *Id.*

Unlike a "brick and mortar outlet" with a specific geographic locale, and unlike the voluntary physical mailing of material from one geographic location to another, as in *Miller*, the uncontroverted facts indicate that the Web is not geographically constrained. See *Reno III*, 31 F. Supp. 2d at 482–92; *American Libraries*, 969 F. Supp. at 169 ("geography, however, is a virtually meaningless construct on the Internet"). Indeed, and of extreme significance, is the fact, as found by the District Court, that Web publishers are without any means to limit access to their sites based on the geographic location of particular Internet users. As soon as information is published on a Web site, it is accessible to all other Web visitors. See *American Libraries*, 969 F. Supp. at 166; *Reno III*, 31 F. Supp. 2d at 483. Current technology prevents Web publishers from circumventing particular jurisdictions or limiting their site's content "from entering any [specific] geographic community." *Reno III*, 31 F. Supp. 2d at 484. This key difference necessarily affects our analysis in attempting to define what contemporary community standards should or could mean in a medium without geographic boundaries.

In expressing its concern over the wholly unprecedented broad coverage of the CDA's scope, the Supreme Court has already noted that because of the peculiar geography-free nature of cyberspace, a "community standards" test would essentially require every Web communication to abide by the most restrictive community's standards. See *Reno II*, 521 U.S. at 877–78. Similarly, to avoid liability under COPA, affected Web publishers would either need to severely censor their publications or implement an age or credit card verification system whereby any material that might be deemed harmful by the most puritan of communities in any state is shielded behind such a verification system. Shielding such vast amounts of material behind verification systems would prevent access to protected material by any adult seventeen or over without the necessary age verification credentials. Moreover, it would completely bar access to those materials to all minors under seventeen—even if the material would not otherwise have been deemed "harmful" to them in their respective geographic communities.

The government argues that subjecting Web publishers to varying community standards is not constitutionally problematic or, for that matter, unusual. The government notes that there are numerous cases in which the courts have already subjected the same conduct to varying community standards, depending on the community in which the conduct occurred. For example, the Supreme Court has stated that "distributors of allegedly obscene materials may be subjected to varying community standards in the various federal judicial districts into which they transmit the material [but that] does not render a federal statute unconstitutional because of the failure of the application of uniform national standards of obscenity." *Hamling v. United States,* 418 U.S. 87, 106, 41 L. Ed. 2d 590, 94 S. Ct. 2887 (1974). Similarly, the government cites to the "dial-a-porn" cases in which the Supreme Court has held that even if the "audience is comprised of different communities with different local standards" the company providing the obscene material "ultimately bears the burden of complying with the prohibition on obscene messages" under each community's respective standard. *Sable Comm. of California v. FCC,* 492 U.S. 115, 125–26, 106 L. Ed. 2d 93, 109 S. Ct. 2829 (1989).

These cases, however, are easily distinguished from the present case. In each of those cases, the defendants had the ability to control the distribution of controversial material with respect to the geographic communities into which they released it. Therefore, the defendants could limit their exposure to liability by avoiding those communities with particularly restrictive standards, while continuing to provide the controversial material in more liberal-minded communities. For example, the pornographer in *Hamling* could have chosen not to mail unsolicited sexually explicit material to certain communities while continuing to mail them to others. Similarly, the telephone pornographers ("dial-a-porn") in *Sable* could have screened their incoming calls and then only accepted a call if its point of origination was from a community with standards of decency that were not offended by the content of their pornographic telephone messages.n20

By contrast, Web publishers have no such comparable control. Web publishers cannot restrict access to their site based on the geographic locale of the Internet user visiting their site. In fact, "an Internet user cannot foreclose access to . . . work from certain states or send differing versions of . . . communication[s] to different jurisdictions. . . . The Internet user has no ability to bypass any particular state." *American Libraries Ass'n v. Pataki,* 969 F. Supp. 160 (S.D.N.Y. 1997). As a result, unlike telephone or postal mail pornographers, Web publishers of material that may be harmful to minors must "comply with the regulation imposed by the State with the most stringent standard or [entirely] forego Internet communication of the message that might or might not subject [the publisher] to prosecution." *Id.*

To minimize this distinction between Web publishers and all other forms of communication that contain material that is harmful to minors, the Government cites to one Sixth Circuit case—presently the only case in which a court has applied a "community standards" test in the context of the electronic medium. See *United States v. Thomas*, 74 F.3d 701 (6th Cir. 1996). The *Thomas* court determined that whether the material on the defendant's electronic bulletin board is harmful must be judged by the standards of each individual community wherein the disputed material was received, even if the standards in each of the recipient communities varied one from the next, and even if the material was acceptable in the community from which it was sent. See *id* at 711. Despite the "electronic medium" in which electronic bulletin boards are found, *Thomas* is inapposite inasmuch as electronic bulletin boards, just as telephones, regular mail and other brick and mortar outlets, are very different creatures from that of the Web as a whole. *Thomas* itself recognized this difference, and by limiting its holding accordingly, completely undercuts the government's argument, stating explicitly that:

> Defendants and Amicus Curiae appearing on their behalf argue that the computer technology used here requires a new definition of community, i.e., one that is based on the broad-ranging connections among people in cyberspace rather than the geographic locale of the federal judicial district of the criminal trial. . . . Therefore, they contend . . . [bulletin board publishers] will be forced to censor their material so as not to run afoul of the standards of the community with the most restrictive standards. Defendants' First Amendment issue, however, is not implicated by the facts of this case. This is not a situation where the bulletin board operator had no knowledge or control over the jurisdictions where materials were distributed for downloading or printing. Access to the Defendants' [bulletin board] was limited. Membership was necessary and applications were submitted and screened before passwords were issued and materials were distributed. Thus, Defendants had in place methods to limit user access in jurisdictions where the risk of a finding of obscenity was greater than in California. . . . If Defendants did not wish to subject themselves to liability in jurisdictions with less tolerant standards for determining obscenity, they could have refused to give passwords to members in those districts, thus precluding the risk of liability. . . . Thus, under the facts of this case, there is no need for this court to adopt a new definition of "community" for use in obscenity prosecutions involving electronic bulletin boards. This court's decision is guided by one of the cardinal rules governing the federal courts, i.e., never reach constitutional questions not squarely presented by the facts of a case. *Id.* at 711–12.

Thus, it is clear that *Thomas* fails to support the government's position. Indeed, no federal court has yet ruled on whether the Web/Internet may be constitutionally regulated in light of differing community standards.

Our concern with COPA's adoption of *Miller's* "contemporary community standards" test by which to determine whether material is harmful to minors is with respect to its overbreadth in the context of the Web medium. Because no technology currently exists by which Web publishers may avoid liability, such publishers would necessarily be compelled to abide by the "standards of the community most likely to be offended by the message," *Reno II*, 521 U.S. at 877–78, even if the same material would not have been deemed harmful to minors in all other communities. Moreover, by restricting their publications to meet the more stringent standards of less liberal communities, adults whose constitutional rights permit them to view such materials would be unconstitutionally deprived of those rights. Thus, this result imposes an overreaching burden and restriction on constitutionally protected speech.n21

We recognize that invalidating a statute because it is overbroad is "strong medicine." *Broadrick v. Oklahoma*, 413 U.S. 601, 613, 37 L. Ed. 2d 830, 93 S. Ct. 2908 (1972). As such, before concluding that a statute is unconstitutionally overbroad, we seek to determine if the statute is " 'readily susceptible' to a narrowing construction that would make it constitutional . . . [because courts] will not rewrite a . . . law to conform it to constitutional requirements." *Virginia v. American Booksellers Ass'n*, 484 U.S. 383, 397, 98 L. Ed. 2d 782, 108 S. Ct. 636 (1988) (quoting *Erznoznik v. City of Jacksonville*, 422 U.S. 205, 45 L. Ed. 2d 125, 95 S. Ct. 2268 (1975)). See also *Broadrick*, 413 U.S. at 613; *Forsyth County v. Nationalist Movement*, 505 U.S. 123, 130, 120 L. Ed. 2d 101, 112 S. Ct. 2395 (1992); *Shea*, 930 F. Supp. 916 at 939.

Two possible ways to limit the interpretation of COPA are (a) assigning a narrow meaning to the language of the statute itself, or (b) deleting that portion of the statute that is unconstitutional, while preserving the remainder of the statute intact. See, *e.g.*, *Brockett v. Spokane Arcades*, 472 U.S. 491, 502, 86 L. Ed. 2d 394, 105 S. Ct. 2794 (1985); *Shea*, 930 F. Supp. at 939. We therefore turn our attention to whether either limiting construction is feasible here.

The government, in attempting to make use of the first of these salvaging mechanisms, suggests that we should interpret narrowly the "contemporary community standards" language in COPA as an "adult" rather than as a "geographic" standard. The House Report itself suggests this construction to sidestep the potential constitutional problems raised by the Supreme Court in interpreting the CDA's use of a "community standards" phrase. Congress explained:

> The committee intends for the definition of material harmful to minors to parallel the *Ginsberg* and *Miller* definitions of obscenity and harmful to minors. . . . In essence, the Committee intends to adopt the "variable obscenity" standard for minors. The Committee recognizes that the applicability of community standards in the context of the Web is controversial, but understands it as an 'adult' standard, rather than a "geographic" standard, and one that is reasonably constant among adults in America with respect to what is suitable for minors. . . . .Thus, the person posting the material is engaged in interstate commerce and is subjecting himself to the jurisdiction of all communities in a manner similar to the way obscenity laws apply today. H.R. Rep. No. 105-775 at 28 (1998).

Congress reiterated this very position in its amicus brief stating: "COPA adopted a non-geographic, adult age community standard for judging the prurience and offensiveness prongs of the Harmful to Minors test." Brief of Members of Congress as *Amici Curiae* at 16.

Despite the government's effort to salvage this clause of COPA from unconstitutionality, we have before us no evidence to suggest that adults everywhere in America would share the same standards for determining what is harmful to minors. To the contrary, it is significant to us that throughout case law, community standards have always been interpreted as a geographic standard without uniformity. See, *e.g.*, *American Libraries Ass'n v. Pataki*, 969 F. Supp. 160, 182–83 (S.D.N.Y. 1997) ("Courts have long recognized, however, that there is no single 'prevailing community standard' in the United States. Thus, even were all 50 states to enact laws that were verbatim copies of the New York [obscenity] Act, Internet users would still be subject to discordant responsibilities.").

In fact, *Miller*, the very case from which the government derives its "community standards" concept, has made clear that community standards are to be construed in a localized geographic context. "People in different States vary in their tastes and attitudes and this diversity is not to be strangled by the absolutism of imposed uniformity." *Miller* 413 U.S. at 33. Even more directly, the Supreme Court stated in *Miller* that "our nation is simply too big and too diverse for this Court to reasonably expect that such standards [of what is patently offensive] could be articulated for all 50 states in a single formulation. . . . To require a State to structure obscenity proceedings around evidence of a national 'community standard' would be an exercise in futility." *Id.* at 30. We therefore conclude that the interpretation of "contemporary community standards" is not "readily susceptible" to a narrowing construction of "adult" rather than "geographic" standard.

With respect to the second salvaging mechanism, it is an " 'elementary principle that the same statute may be in part constitutional and in part unconstitutional, and that if the parts are wholly independent of each other, that which is constitutional may stand while that which is unconstitutional will be rejected.' " *Brockett v. Spokane Arcades, Inc.,* 472 U.S. 491, 502, 86 L. Ed. 2d 394, 105 S. Ct. 2794 (1985) (quoting *Allen v. Louisiana,* 103 U.S. 80, 83–84, 26 L. Ed. 318 (1881)). As a result, if it is possible for a court to identify a particular part of the statute that is unconstitutional, and by striking only that language the court could leave the remainder of the statute intact and within the intent of Congress, courts should do so. See *Alaska Airlines, Inc. v. Brock,* 480 U.S. 678, 684–85, 94 L. Ed. 2d 661, 107 S. Ct. 1476 (1987).

Here, however, striking "contemporary community standards" from COPA is not likely to succeed in salvaging COPA's constitutionality as this standard is an integral part of the statute, permeating and influencing the whole of the statute. We see no means by which to excise those "unconstitutional" elements of the statute from those that are constitutional (assuming for the moment, without deciding, that the remaining clauses of COPA are held to be constitutional). This is particularly so in a preliminary injunction context when we are convinced that the very test or standard that COPA has established to determine what is harmful to minors is more likely than not to be held unconstitutional. See *Brockett,* 472 U.S. at 504–05.

Our foregoing discussion [demonstrates] that under either approach—of narrowing construction or deleting an unconstitutional element—COPA is not "readily susceptible" to a construction that would make it constitutional. We agree with the Second Circuit that "the State may not regulate at all if it turns out that even the least restrictive means of regulation is still unreasonable when its limitations on freedom of speech are balanced against the benefits gained from those limitations." *Carlin Communications, Inc. v. FCC,* 837 F.2d 546, 555 (2d Cir. 1988). As regulation under existing technology is unreasonable here, we conclude that with respect to this first prong of our preliminary injunction analysis, it is more likely than not that COPA will be found unconstitutional on the merits.n22

Our holding in no way ignores or questions the general applicability of the holding in *Miller* with respect to "contemporary community standards." We remain satisfied that *Miller's* "community standards" test continues to be a useful and viable tool in contexts other than the Internet and the Web under present technology. *Miller* itself was designed to address the mailing of unsolicited sexually explicit material in violation of California law, where a publisher could control the community receiving the publication. *Miller,* however, has no applicability to the Internet and the Web, where Web publishers are currently without the ability to control the geographic scope of the recipients of their communications. See *Reno II,* 521 U.S. at 889 (O'Connor, J., concurring in judgment in part and dissenting in part) (noting that the "twin characteristics of geography and identity" differentiate the world of *Ginsberg* [and *Miller*] from that of the Internet.).

B. Irreparable Harm By Denial of Relief

The second prong of our preliminary injunction analysis requires us to consider "whether the movant will be irreparably harmed by denial of the relief." *Allegheny Energy, Inc. v. DQE, Inc.* 171 F.3d 153, 158 (3d Cir. 1999). Generally, "in a First Amendment challenge, a plaintiff who meets the first prong of the test for a preliminary injunction will almost certainly meet the second, since irreparable injury normally arises out of the deprivation of speech rights." *Reno I,* 929 F. Supp. 824 at 866. This case is no exception.

If a preliminary injunction were not to issue, COPA-affected Web publishers would most assuredly suffer irreparable harm—the curtailment of their constitutionally protected right to free speech. As the Supreme Court has clearly stated, "the loss of First Amendment freedoms, for even minimal periods of time, unquestionably constitutes irreparable injury." *Elrod v. Burns,* 427 U.S. 347, 373, 49 L. Ed. 2d 547, 96 S. Ct. 2673 (1976). We, therefore, conclude that this element of our preliminary injunction analysis has been satisfied.

C. Injury Outweighs Harm

The third prong of our preliminary injunction analysis requires us to consider "whether granting preliminary relief will result in even greater harm to the nonmoving party." *Allegheny Inc. v. DQE,* Inc., 171 F.3d 153, 158 (3d Cir. 1999). We are convinced that in balancing the parties' respective interests, COPA's threatened constraint on constitutionally protected free speech far outweighs the damage that would be imposed by our failure to affirm this preliminary injunction. We are also aware that without a preliminary injunction,

Web publishers subject to COPA would immediately be required to censor constitutionally protected speech for adults, or incur substantial financial costs to implement COPA's affirmative defenses.n23 Therefore, we affirm the District Court's holding that plaintiffs sufficiently met their burden in establishing this third prong of the preliminary injunction analysis.

D. Public Interest

As the fourth and final element of our preliminary injunction analysis, we consider "whether granting the preliminary relief will be in the public interest." *Allegheny Inc. v. DQE, Inc.*, 171 F.3d 153, 158 (3d Cir. 1999). Curtailing constitutionally protected speech will not advance the public interest, and "neither the Government nor the public generally can claim an interest in the enforcement of an unconstitutional law." *Reno I*, 929 F. Supp. at 866. Having met this final element of our preliminary injunction analysis, the District Court properly granted the ACLU's petition for a preliminary injunction.

III. Conclusion

Due to current technological limitations, COPA—Congress' laudatory attempt to achieve its compelling objective of protecting minors from harmful material on the World Wide Web—is more likely than not to be found unconstitutional as overbroad on the merits.n24 Because the ACLU has met its burden in establishing all four of the necessary elements to obtain a preliminary injunction, and the District Court properly exercised its discretion in issuing the preliminary injunction, we will affirm the District Court's order.

In so affirming, we approvingly reiterate the sentiments aptly noted by the District Court: "Sometimes we must make decisions that we do not like. We make them because they are right, right in the sense that the law and the Constitution, as we see them, compel the result." *Reno III*, 31 F. Supp. 2d at 498.n25 We also express our confidence and firm conviction that developing technology will soon render the "community standards" challenge moot, thereby making congressional regulation to protect minors from harmful material on the Web constitutionally practicable. Indeed, in the context of dealing with technology to prevent the "bleeding" of cable transmissions, the Supreme Court in *United States v. Playboy Entertainment Group, Inc.*, 529 U.S. 803, 120 S. Ct. 1878, 146 L. Ed. 2d 865, 2000 WL 646196 at *4 (U.S. 2000) recognized, as do we, that "technology may one day provide another solution."

Therefore, we will affirm the District Court's order dated February 1, 1999, issuing a preliminary injunction.

MAINSTREAM LOUDOUN ET AL., PLAINTIFFS, V. BOARD OF
TRUSTEES OF THE LOUDOUN COUNTY LIBRARY ET AL.,
DEFENDANTS

Civil Action No. 97-2049-A

UNITED STATES DISTRICT COURT FOR THE EASTERN
DISTRICT OF VIRGINIA, ALEXANDRIA DIVISION

2 F. Supp. 2d 783; 1998 U.S. Dist. LEXIS 4725

April 7, 1998 Decided

DISPOSITION:

Defendants' Motion to Dismiss the Individual Defendants GRANTED, and
their Motion to Dismiss for Failure to State a Claim GRANTED IN PART
and DENIED IN PART. Defendants' Motion in the Alternative for Summary
Judgment DENIED.

. . .

OPINION BY:

Leonie M. Brinkema, United States District Judge

OPINION:

Memorandum Opinion and Order

Before the Court are defendants' Motion to Dismiss the Individual Defendants and Motion to Dismiss for Failure to State a Claim or, in the Alternative, for Summary Judgment, in a case of first impression, involving the
applicability of the First Amendment's free speech clause to public libraries'
content-based restrictions on Internet access.

I. Background

The plaintiffs in this case are an association, Mainstream Loudoun, and ten individual plaintiffs, all of whom are both members of Mainstream Loudoun and adult patrons of Loudoun County public libraries. Defendants are the Board of Trustees of the Loudoun County Public Library, five individual Board members, and Douglas Henderson, Loudoun County's Director of Library Services. The Loudoun County public library system has six branches and provides patrons with access to the Internet and the World Wide Web. Under state law, the "management and control" of this library system is vested in a Board of Trustees (the "Library Board"). See Va. Code Ann. § 42.1-35. Library Board members are appointed by County officials and are not elected. See *id.* In addition to their management and control duties, Virginia Code § 42.1-35 directs the Library Board to "adopt such bylaws, rules and regulations for their own guidance and for the government of the free public library system as may be expedient."

On October 20, 1997, the Library Board voted to adopt a "Policy on Internet Sexual Harassment" (the "Policy"), which requires that "site-blocking software . . . be installed on all [library] computers" so as to: "a. block child pornography and obscene material (hard-core pornography)"; and "b. block material deemed Harmful to Juveniles under applicable Virginia statutes and legal precedents (soft-core pornography)." To implement the Policy, the Library Board chose "X-Stop," a commercial software product intended to limit access to sites deemed to violate the Policy.

Plaintiffs allege that the Policy impermissibly blocks their access to protected speech such as the Quaker Home Page, the Zero Population Growth Web site, and the site for the American Association of University Women–Maryland. Complaint PP96-105. They also claim that there are no clear criteria for blocking decisions and that defendants maintain an unblocking policy that unconstitutionally chills plaintiffs' receipt of constitutionally protected materials. Complaint PP92, 95, 127–29.

Based on the above allegations, plaintiffs bring this action under 42 U.S.C. § 1983 against the Library Board and against five individual Library Board members in both their personal and official capacities, and Director of Library Services Douglas Henderson in his official capacity. Plaintiffs allege that the Policy imposes an unconstitutional restriction on their right to access protected speech on the Internet, and seek declaratory and injunctive relief, as well as costs and attorneys' fees pursuant to 42 U.S.C. § 1988.n1

II. Immunity Issues

. . .

B. *Communications Decency Act Immunity*

Defendants also claim that they are immune from suit under section 509 of the Telecommunications Act of 1996, now codified at 47 U.S.C. § 230. Section 230 is entitled "Protection for private blocking and screening of offensive material," and provides at § 230(c)(2) that:

> No provider or user of an interactive computer service shall be held liable on account of . . . any action voluntarily taken in good faith to restrict access to or availability of material that the provider or user considers to be obscene, lewd, lascivious, filthy, excessively violent, harassing, or otherwise objectionable, whether or not such material is constitutionally protected.

The Act defines "interactive computer service" to include "a service or system that provides access to the Internet [that is] offered by libraries or educational institutions." 47 U.S.C. § 230(e)(2). Based on the above language, defendants argue that they are absolutely immune from suit for their decision to promulgate and enforce the Policy.

Although defendants' interpretation of § 230(a)(2) is facially attractive, it is not supported by that section's legislative history or relevant case law. At the beginning of § 230, Congress states that "it is the policy of the United States . . . to preserve the vibrant and competitive free market that presently exists for the Internet and other interactive computer services, unfettered by federal or state regulation." 47 U.S.C. § 230(b)(2). Interpreting § 230, the Fourth Circuit has explained that:

> The purpose of [§ 230] statutory immunity is not difficult to discern. Congress recognized the threat that tort-based lawsuits pose to freedom of speech in the new and burgeoning Internet medium. The imposition of tort liability on service providers for the communications of others represented, for Congress, simply another form of intrusive government regulation of speech. Section 230 was enacted, in part, to maintain the robust nature of Internet communication and, accordingly, to keep government interference in the medium to a minimum.

Zeran v. America Online, 129 F.3d 327, 330 (4th Cir. 1997). The Fourth Circuit went on to explain that "another important purpose of § 230 was to encourage service providers to self-regulate the dissemination of offensive materials over their services." *Id.* at 331. Thus, as its name implies, § 230 was enacted to minimize state regulation of Internet speech by encouraging private content providers to self-regulate against offensive material; § 230 was not enacted to insulate government regulation of Internet speech from judicial review. Even if § 230 were construed to apply to public libraries, defendants cite no authority to suggest that the "tort-based" immunity to "civil liability" described by § 230 would bar the instant action, which is for declaratory and injunctive relief. See 47 U.S.C. § 230(a)(2); *Zeran*, 129 F.3d at 330. We therefore hold that 47 U.S.C. § 230 does not bar this action. . . .

IV. Plaintiffs' First Amendment Claim

In their Motion to Dismiss for Failure to State a Claim, or, in the Alternative, for Summary Judgment, defendants concede that the Policy prohibits access to speech on the basis of its content. See Def. Brief at 11. However, defendants argue that the "First Amendment does not in any way limit the decisions of a public library on whether to provide access to information on the Internet." Def. Brief at 2. Indeed, at oral argument, defendants went so far as to claim that a public library could constitutionally prohibit access to speech simply because it was authored by African-Americans, or because it espoused a particular political viewpoint, for example pro-Republican. See Feb. 27, 1998 Hearing Transcript at 48. Thus, the central question before this Court is whether a public library may, without violating the First Amendment, enforce content-based restrictions on access to Internet speech.

No cases directly address this issue. However, the parties agree that the most analogous authority on this issue is *Board of Education v. Pico*, 457 U.S. 853, 73 L. Ed. 2d 435, 102 S. Ct. 2799 (1982), in which the Supreme Court reviewed the decision of a local board of education to remove certain books from a high school library based on the board's belief that the books were "anti-American, anti-Christian, anti-Semitic, and just plain filthy." *Id.* at 856. The Second Circuit had reversed the district court's grant of summary judgment to the school board on plaintiff's First Amendment claim. A sharply-divided Court voted to affirm the Court of Appeal's decision to remand the case for a determination of the school board's motives. However, the Court did not render a majority opinion. Justice Brennan, joined by three Justices, wrote what is commonly referred to as the "plurality" opinion.

Justice Brennan held that the First Amendment necessarily limits the government's right to remove materials on the basis of their content from a high school library. See *id.* at 864–69 (plurality op.). Justice Brennan reasoned that the right to receive information is inherent in the right to speak and that "the State may not, consistently with the spirit of the First Amendment, contract the spectrum of available knowledge." *Id.* at 866 (quoting *Griswold v. Connecticut,* 381 U.S. 479, 482, 14 L. Ed. 2d 510, 85 S. Ct. 1678 (1965)); see also *Stanley v. Georgia,* 394 U.S. 557, 564, 22 L. Ed. 2d 542, 89 S. Ct. 1243 (1969) ("the Constitution protects the right to receive information and ideas"). Justice Brennan explained that this principle was particularly important given the special role of the school's library as a locus for free and independent inquiry. See *id.* 457 U.S. at 869. At the same time, Justice Brennan recognized that public high schools play a crucial inculcative role in "the preparation of individuals for participation as citizens" and are therefore entitled to great discretion "to establish and apply their curriculum in such a way as to transmit community values." *Id.* at 863–64 (quoting *Ambach v. Norwick,* 441 U.S. 68, 76-77, 60 L. Ed. 2d 49, 99 S. Ct. 1589 (1979) (internal quotation marks omitted)). Accordingly, Justice Brennan held that the school board members could not remove books "simply because they dislike the ideas contained [in them]," thereby "prescribing what shall be orthodox in politics, nationalism, religion, or other matters of opinion," but that the board might remove books for reasons of educational suitability, for example pervasive vulgarity. *Id.* 457 U.S. at 872 (quoting *West Va. Bd. of Educ. v. Barnette,* 319 U.S. 624, 642, 87 L. Ed. 1628, 63 S. Ct. 1178 (1943) (internal quotation marks omitted)).

In a concurring opinion, Justice Blackmun focused not on the right to receive information recognized by the plurality, but on the school board's discrimination against disfavored ideas. Justice Blackmun explicitly recognized that Pico's facts invoked two significant, competing interests: the inculcative mission of public high schools and the First Amendment's core proscription against content-based regulation of speech. See *id.* 457 U.S. at 876–79 (Blackmun, J., concurring). Justice Blackmun noted that the State must normally demonstrate a compelling reason for content-based regulation, but that a more limited form of protection should apply in the context of public high schools. See *id.* at 877–78. Balancing the two principles above, Justice Blackmun agreed with the plurality that the school board could not remove books based on mere disapproval of their content but could limit its collection for reasons of educational suitability or budgetary constraint. See *id.* at 879.

Dissenting, Chief Justice Burger, joined by three Justices, concluded that any First Amendment right to receive speech did not affirmatively obligate the government to provide such speech in high school libraries. See *id.* at 888 (Burger, C.J., dissenting). Chief Justice Burger reasoned that although the State could not constitutionally prohibit a speaker from reaching an intended audience, nothing in the First Amendment requires public high schools to act as a conduit for particular speech. See *id.* at 885–89. Chief Justice Burger explained that such an obligation would be inconsistent with public high schools' inculcative mission, which necessarily requires schools to make content-based choices among competing ideas in order to establish a curriculum and educate students. See *id.* at 889.

Defendants contend that the *Pico* plurality opinion has no application to this case because it addressed only decisions to remove materials from libraries and specifically declined to address library decisions to acquire materials. See *id.* at 861–63, 871–72 (plurality op.). Defendants liken the Internet to a vast Interlibrary Loan system, and contend that restricting Internet access to selected materials is merely a decision not to acquire such materials rather than a decision to remove them from a library's collection. As such, defendants argue, the instant case is outside the scope of the *Pico* plurality.

In response, plaintiffs argue that, unlike a library's collection of individual books, the Internet is a "single, integrated system." Pl. Brief at 14 (quoting *ACLU v. Reno*, 929 F. Supp. 824, 838 (E.D. Pa. 1996), aff'd, 138 L. Ed. 2d 874, 117 S. Ct. 2329 (1997). As plaintiffs explain, "though information on the Web is contained in individual computers, the fact that each of these computers is connected to the Internet through [World Wide Web] protocols allows all of the information to become part of a single body of knowledge." Pl. Brief at 15 (quoting *Reno*, 929 F. Supp. at 836). Accordingly, plaintiffs analogize the Internet to a set of encyclopedias, and the Library Board's enactment of the Policy to a decision to "black out" selected articles considered inappropriate for adult and juvenile patrons.

After considering both arguments, we conclude that defendants have misconstrued the nature of the Internet. By purchasing Internet access, each Loudoun library has made all Internet publications instantly accessible to its patrons. Unlike an Interlibrary Loan or outright book purchase, no appreciable expenditure of library time or resources is required to make a particular Internet publication available to a library patron. In contrast, a library must actually expend resources to restrict Internet access to a publication that is otherwise immediately available. In effect, by purchasing one such publication, the library has purchased them all. The Internet therefore more closely resembles plaintiffs' analogy of a collection of encyclopedias from which defendants have laboriously redacted portions deemed unfit for library patrons. As such, the Library Board's action is more appropriately characterized as a removal decision. We therefore conclude that the principles discussed in the *Pico* plurality are relevant and apply to the Library Board's decision to promulgate and enforce the Policy.

Plaintiffs also contend that the plurality's decision in *Pico* establishes a blanket rule that removal decisions by libraries may not be resolved on summary judgment. We find plaintiffs' reading of *Pico* to be oversimplistic. It is true that a majority of the *Pico* Court voted to remand the case for a determination of the school board's motives, impliedly rejecting the unfettered discretion defendants claim. See *id.* at 875. At the same time, however, a majority of the Court could not agree on the degree of discretion available to school libraries. See *id.* at 856 (plurality op.); 875 (Blackmun, J., concurring); cf. *id.* at 883 (White, J., concurring). Nor did any of the *Pico* Justices directly address the special circumstances that obtain in public libraries. It would therefore be inappropriate for this Court to deny defendants' Motion without first determining the scope of discretion available to the Library Board to remove materials on the basis of their content.

Defendants argue that any limitation on their discretion to remove materials would force them to act as an unwilling conduit of information, and urge this Court to adopt the position of the *Pico* dissent. Defendants interpret the dissent to mean that they are entitled to unfettered discretion in deciding what materials to make available to library patrons.

Adopting defendants' position, however, would require this Court to ignore the *Pico* plurality's decision to remand the case, as discussed above. Moreover, all of the *Pico* Justices, including the dissenters, recognized that any discretion accorded to school libraries was uniquely tied to the public school's role as educator. See *id.* at 863–64, 869–71 (plurality op.); 875–76, 879 (Blackmun, J., concurring) ("Certainly, the unique environment of the school places substantial limits on the extent to which official decisions may be restrained by First Amendment values."); cf. *id.* at 889–92 (Burger, C.J., dissenting) ("Whatever role the government might play as a conduit of information, schools in particular ought not be made a slavish courier of the material of third parties. . . . How are 'fundamental values' to be inculcated except

by having school boards make content-based decisions about the appropriateness of retaining materials in the school library and curriculum[?]");
909–10 (Rehnquist, J., dissenting) ("When it acts as an educator . . . the government is engaged in inculcating social values and knowledge in relatively impressionable young people. . . . In short, actions by the government as educator do not raise the same First Amendment concerns as actions by the government as sovereign."); 921 (O'Connor, J., dissenting) (stating that "in this case the government is acting in its special role as educator"). Of even more significance to our case is Justice Rehnquist's observation that high school libraries must be treated differently from public libraries. See *id.* at 915 (Rehnquist, J., dissenting) ("Unlike university or public libraries, elementary and secondary school libraries are not designed for freewheeling inquiry."). Indeed, Chief Justice Burger and Justice Rehnquist justified giving public schools broad discretion to remove books in part by noting that such materials remained available in public libraries. See *id.* at 892 (Burger, C.J., dissenting) ("Books may be acquired from . . . public libraries, or other alternative sources unconnected with the unique environment of the local public schools."); 915 (Rehnquist, J., dissenting) ("The most obvious reason that petitioners' removal of the books did not violate respondents' right to receive information is the ready availability of the books elsewhere. . . . The books may be borrowed from a public library."). Accordingly, neither the dissent nor the plurality of *Pico* can be said to support defendants' argument that public libraries enjoy unfettered discretion to remove materials from their collections.

To the extent that *Pico* applies to this case, we conclude that it stands for the proposition that the First Amendment applies to, and limits, the discretion of a public library to place content-based restrictions on access to constitutionally protected materials within its collection. Consistent with the mandate of the First Amendment, a public library, "like other enterprises operated by the State, may not be run in such a manner as to 'prescribe what shall be orthodox in politics, nationalism, religion, or other matters of opinion.' " *Id.* at 876 (Blackmun, J., concurring) (quoting *Barnette*, 319 U.S. at 642).

Furthermore, the factors which justified giving high school libraries broad discretion to remove materials in *Pico* are not present in this case. The plaintiffs in this case are adults rather than children. Children, whose minds and values are still developing, have traditionally been afforded less First Amendment protection, particularly within the context of public high schools. See

Tinker v. Des Moines Sch. Dist., 393 U.S. 503, 506, 21 L. Ed. 2d 731, 89 S. Ct. 733 (1969). In contrast, adults are deemed to have acquired the maturity needed to participate fully in a democratic society, and their right to speak and receive speech is entitled to full First Amendment protection. Accordingly, adults are entitled to receive categories of speech, for example "pervasively vulgar" speech, which may be inappropriate for children. See *Reno v. ACLU*, 138 L. Ed. 2d 874, 117 S. Ct. 2329, 2346 (1997); *Sable Communications v. FCC*, 492 U.S. 115, 126, 106 L. Ed. 2d 93, 109 S. Ct. 2829 (1989).

More importantly, the tension Justice Blackmun recognized between the inculcative role of high schools and the First Amendment's prohibition on content-based regulation of speech does not exist here. See *Pico*, 457 U.S. at 876–80 (Blackmun, J., concurring). Public libraries lack the inculcative mission that is the guiding purpose of public high schools. Instead, public libraries are places of freewheeling and independent inquiry. See *id.* at 914 (Rehnquist, J., dissenting). Adult library patrons are presumed to have acquired already the "fundamental values" needed to act as citizens, and have come to the library to pursue their personal intellectual interests rather than the curriculum of a high school classroom. As such, no curricular motive justifies a public library's decision to restrict access to Internet materials on the basis of their content.

Finally, the unique advantages of Internet speech eliminate any resource-related rationale libraries might otherwise have for engaging in content-based discrimination. The Supreme Court has analogized the Internet to a "vast library including millions of readily available and indexed publications," the content of which "is as diverse as human thought." *Reno II*, 117 S. Ct. at 2335. Unlike more traditional libraries, however, there is no marginal cost associated with acquiring Internet publications. Instead, all, or nearly all, Internet publications are jointly available for a single price. Indeed, it costs a library more to restrict the content of its collection by means of blocking software than it does for the library to offer unrestricted access to all Internet publications. Nor do Internet publications, which exist only in "cyberspace," take up shelf space or require physical maintenance of any kind. Accordingly, considerations of cost or physical resources cannot justify a public library's decision to restrict access to Internet materials. Cf. *Pico*, 457 U.S. at 909 (Rehnquist, J., dissenting) (budgetary considerations force schools to choose some books over others); 879 n.1 (Blackmun, J., concurring) (same).

In sum, there is "no basis for qualifying the level of First Amendment scrutiny" that must be applied to a public library's decision to restrict access to Internet publications. *Reno II*, 117 S. Ct. at 2344. We are therefore left with the First Amendment central tenet that content-based restrictions on speech must be justified by a compelling governmental interest and must be narrowly tailored to achieve that end. See *Simon & Schuster v. Members of the N.Y. State Crime Victims Bd.*, 502 U.S. 105, 118, 116 L. Ed. 2d 476, 112 S. Ct. 501 (1991). This principle was recently affirmed within the context of Internet speech. See *Reno II*, 117 S. Ct. at 2343–48. Accordingly, we hold that the Library Board may not adopt and enforce content-based restrictions on access to protected Internet speech absent a compelling state interest and means narrowly drawn to achieve that end.

This holding does not obligate defendants to act as unwilling conduits of information, because the Library Board need not provide access to the Internet at all. Having chosen to provide access, however, the Library Board may not thereafter selectively restrict certain categories of Internet speech because it disfavors their content. In accord with this holding is *Lamont*, discussed supra, in which the Court held that the Post Office could not constitutionally restrict access to speech it considered "communist propaganda," stating that " 'the United States may give up the post-office when it sees fit, but while it carries it on the use of the mails is almost as much a part of free speech as the right to use our tongues.' " *Lamont*, 381 U.S. at 305 (quoting *Milwaukee Soc. Dem. Pub. Co. v. Burleson*, 255 U.S. 407, 437, 65 L. Ed. 704, 41 S. Ct. 352 (1921) (Holmes, J., dissenting)); see *id.* 381 U.S. at 310 ("If the Government wishes to withdraw a subsidy or a privilege, it must do so by means and on terms which do not endanger First Amendment rights.") (Brennan, J., concurring). Similarly, in this case, the Library Board need not offer Internet access, but, having chosen to provide it, must operate the service within the confines of the First Amendment.

A. Obscenity, Child Pornography, and Speech "Harmful to Juveniles"

Having determined that a public library must satisfy strict scrutiny before it may engage in content-based regulation of protected speech, we now consider the speech regulated by the Policy. The Policy prohibits access to three types of speech: obscenity, child pornography, and materials deemed "harmful to juveniles." Complaint Ex. 1. Obscenity and child pornography are not entitled to the protections of the First Amendment, and the government may legitimately restrict access to such materials. See *New York v. Ferber,* 458 U.S. 747, 73 L. Ed. 2d 1113, 102 S. Ct. 3348 (1982) (child pornography); *Miller v. California,* 413 U.S. 15, 37 L. Ed. 2d 419, 93 S. Ct. 2607 (1973) (obscenity). Indeed, "transmitting obscenity and child pornography, whether via the Internet or other means, is already illegal under federal law for both adults and juveniles." *Reno II,* 117 S. Ct. at 2348 n.44. In the instant case, however, plaintiffs allege that the X-Stop filtering software chosen by defendants restricts many publications which are not obscene or pornographic, including materials unrelated to sex altogether, such as the Quaker's Web site. See Complaint PP96–105. Moreover, plaintiffs allege that X-Stop fails to block access to pornographic materials arguably covered by the Policy. See Complaint P127. Most importantly, plaintiffs allege that the decision as to which materials to block is made by a California corporation based on secret criteria not disclosed even to defendants, criteria which may or may not bear any relation to legal definitions of obscenity or child pornography. See Complaint PP95, 128–29. As such, plaintiffs argue that the means called for by the Policy are not narrowly tailored to any legitimate interest defendants may have in regulating obscenity and child pornography.

The Policy also prohibits access to materials which are "deemed Harmful to Juveniles under applicable Virginia statutes and legal precedents." This appears to be a reference to Virginia Code § 18.2-390, which defines materials "Harmful to Juveniles" to include sexual content that:

> (a) predominately appeals to the prurient, shameful or morbid interest of juveniles, (b) is patently offensive to prevailing standards in the adult community as a whole with respect to what is suitable material for juveniles, and (c) is, when taken as a whole, lacking in serious literary, artistic, political or scientific value for juveniles.

Plaintiffs allege that the Policy improperly limits adult Internet speech to what is fit for children. In support, plaintiffs cite *Reno II,* 117 S. Ct. at 2329. In *Reno,* the Supreme Court held that a content-based Internet regulation intended to prevent the transmission of material harmful to minors was unconstitutional because it suppressed speech adults were constitutionally entitled to send and receive. The Court stated:

> It is true that we have repeatedly recognized the governmental interest in protecting children from harmful materials. But that interest does not jus-

tify an unnecessarily broad suppression of speech addressed to adults. As we have explained, the Government may not "reduce the adult population . . . to . . . only what is fit for children."

Id. 117 S. Ct. at 2346 (quoting *Denver Area Telecomm. Consortium v. FCC*, 518 U.S. 727, 116 S. Ct. 2374, 2393, 135 L. Ed. 2d 888 (1996)). (notes omitted) The Court went on to cite *Bolger v. Youngs Drug Products Corp.*, 463 U.S. 60, 77 L. Ed. 2d 469, 103 S. Ct. 2875 (1983), for the proposition that: " 'Regardless of the strength of the government's interest' in protecting children, 'the level of discourse reaching a mailbox simply cannot be limited to that which would be suitable for a sandbox.' " *Reno II*, 117 S. Ct. at 2346 (quoting *Bolger*, 463 U.S. at 74–75). Applying *Reno* to the instant case, it is clear that defendants may not, in the interest of protecting children, limit the speech available to adults to what is fit for "juveniles." As plaintiffs point out, even when government regulation of content is undertaken for a legitimate purpose, whether it be to prevent the communication of obscene speech or materials harmful to children, the means it uses must be a "reasonable response to the threat" which will alleviate the harm "in a direct and material way." *Turner Broadcasting v. FCC*, 512 U.S. 622, 624, 129 L. Ed. 2d 497, 114 S. Ct. 2445 (1994). Plaintiffs have adequately alleged a lack of such reasonable means here. As such, plaintiffs have stated a valid First Amendment claim which may go forward.

B. The Unblocking Policy

Defendants contend that, even if the First Amendment limits the Library Board's discretion to remove materials, the unblocking procedure ensures the constitutionality of the Policy because it allows library staff to make certain that only constitutionally unprotected materials are blocked. Under the unblocking policy, library patrons who have been denied access to a site may submit a written request which must include their name, telephone number, and a detailed explanation of why they desire access to the blocked site. The library staff then "decide[s] whether the request should be granted." Def. Brief at 3.n4

Plaintiffs argue that the unblocking procedure constitutes an unconstitutional burden on the right of library patrons to access protected speech, citing *Lamont*, 381 U.S. at 301. The statute at issue in *Lamont* directed the Postmaster General not to deliver "communist propaganda" to postal patrons unless they first returned to the Post Office a card bearing their names and addresses and specifically requesting that such materials be sent to them. See *id.* at 302–04. The Supreme Court held the statute to be "unconstitutional because it required an official act (viz., returning the reply card) as a limitation on the unfettered exercise of the addressees' First Amendment rights." *Id.* at 305. In particular, the Court noted the severe chilling effect of forcing citizens to publicly petition the Government for access to speech it clearly disfavored. See *id.* at 307.

Here, as in *Lamont*, the unblocking policy forces adult patrons to petition the Government for access to otherwise protected speech, for example speech "Harmful to Juveniles." Indeed, the Loudoun County unblocking policy appears more chilling than the restriction at issue in *Lamont*, because it grants library staff standardless discretion to refuse access to protected speech, whereas the statute at issue in *Lamont* required postal employees to grant access requests automatically. As such, defendants' alleged unblocking procedure does not in any way undercut plaintiffs' First Amendment claim.

V. Conclusion

For the reasons set forth above, defendants' Motion to Dismiss the Individual Defendants will be *granted*, and their Motion to Dismiss for Failure to State a Claim will be *granted in part* as to certain plaintiffs and *denied* in all other respects. As to defendants' Motion in the Alternative for Summary Judgment, this Court holds that several material factual issues remain which mandate against summary judgment at this time. These include, but are not limited to, defendants' justification for the Policy, the Internet sites blocked by X-Stop, and the degree of defendants' knowledge of and control over the sites X-Stop blocks. Accordingly, defendants' Motion in the Alternative for Summary Judgment will also be *denied*. An appropriate order will issue.

CHILD ONLINE PROTECTION ACT—COPA

47 U.S.C.S. § 231 *et. seq.* (2000)

§ 231. Restriction of access by minors to materials commercially distributed by means of World Wide Web that are harmful to minors

(a) Requirement to restrict access.

(1) Prohibited conduct. Whoever knowingly and with knowledge of the character of the material, in interstate or foreign commerce by means of the World Wide Web, makes any communication for commercial purposes that is available to any minor and that includes any material that is harmful to minors shall be fined not more than $50,000, imprisoned not more than 6 months, or both.

(2) Intentional violations. In addition to the penalties under paragraph (1), whoever intentionally violates such paragraph shall be subject to a fine of not more than $50,000 for each violation. For purposes of this paragraph, each day of violation shall constitute a separate violation.

(3) Civil penalty. In addition to the penalties under paragraphs (1) and (2), whoever violates paragraph (1) shall be subject to a civil penalty of not more than $50,000 for each violation. For purposes of this paragraph, each day of violation shall constitute a separate violation.

(b) Inapplicability of carriers and other service providers. For purposes of subsection (a), a person shall not be considered to make any communication for commercial purposes to the extent that such person is—

(1) a telecommunications carrier engaged in the provision of a telecommunications service;

(2) a person engaged in the business of providing an Internet access service;

(3) a person engaged in the business of providing an Internet information location tool; or

(4) similarly engaged in the transmission, storage, retrieval, hosting, for-

matting, or translation (or any combination thereof) of a communication made by another person, without selection or alteration of the content of the communication, except that such person's deletion of a particular communication or material made by another person in a manner consistent with subsection (c) or section 230 [47 U.S.C.S. § 230] shall not constitute such selection or alteration of the content of the communication.

(c) Affirmative defense.

(1) Defense. It is an affirmative defense to prosecution under this section that the defendant, in good faith, has restricted access by minors to material that is harmful to minors—

(A) by requiring use of a credit card, debit account, adult access code, or adult personal identification number;

(B) by accepting a digital certificate that verifies age; or

(C) by any other reasonable measures that are feasible under available technology.

(2) Protection for use of defenses. No cause of action may be brought in any court or administrative agency against any person on account of any activity that is not in violation of any law punishable by criminal or civil penalty, and that the person has taken in good faith to implement a defense authorized under this subsection or otherwise to restrict or prevent the transmission of, or access to, a communication specified in this section.

(d) Privacy protection requirements.

(1) Disclosure of information limited. A person making a communication described in subsection (a)—

(A) shall not disclose any information collected for the purposes of restricting access to such communications to individuals 17 years of age or older without the prior written or electronic consent of—

(i) the individual concerned, if the individual is an adult; or

(ii) the individual's parent or guardian, if the individual is under 17 years of age; and

(B) shall take such actions as are necessary to prevent unauthorized access to such information by a person other than the person making such communication and the recipient of such communication.

(2) Exceptions. A person making a communication described in subsection (a) may disclose such information if the disclosure is—

(A) necessary to make the communication or conduct a legitimate business activity related to making the communication; or

(B) made pursuant to a court order authorizing such disclosure.

(e) Definitions. For purposes of this subsection, the following definitions shall apply:

(1) By means of the World Wide Web. The term "by means of the World Wide Web" means by placement of material in a computer server–based file archive so that it is publicly accessible, over the Internet, using hypertext transfer protocol or any successor protocol.

(2) Commercial purposes; engaged in the business.

(A) Commercial purposes. A person shall be considered to make a communication for commercial purposes only if such person is engaged in the business of making such communications.

(B) Engaged in the business. The term "engaged in the business" means that the person who makes a communication, or offers to make a communication, by means of the World Wide Web, that includes any material that is harmful to minors, devotes time, attention, or labor to such activities, as a regular course of such person's trade or business, with the objective of earning a profit as a result of such activities (although it is not necessary that the person make a profit or that the making or offering to make such communications be the person's sole or principal business or source of income). A person may be considered to be engaged in the business of making, by means of the World Wide Web, communications for commercial purposes that include material that is harmful to minors, only if the person knowingly causes the material that is harmful to minors to be posted on the World Wide Web or knowingly solicits such material to be posted on the World Wide Web.

(3) Internet. The term "Internet" means the combination of computer facilities and electromagnetic transmission media, and related equipment and software, comprising the interconnected worldwide network of computer networks that employ the Transmission Control Protocol/Internet Protocol or any successor protocol to transmit information.

(4) Internet access service. The term "Internet access service" means a service that enables users to access content, information, electronic mail, or other services offered over the Internet, and may also include access to proprietary content, information, and other services as part of a package of

services offered to consumers. Such term does not include telecommunications services.

(5) Internet information location tool. The term "Internet information location tool" means a service that refers or links users to an online location on the World Wide Web. Such term includes directories, indices, references, pointers, and hypertext links.

(6) Material that is harmful to minors. The term "material that is harmful to minors" means any communication, picture, image, graphic image file, article, recording, writing, or other matter of any kind that is obscene or that—

(A) the average person, applying contemporary community standards, would find, taking the material as a whole and with respect to minors, is designed to appeal to, or is designed to pander to, the prurient interest;

(B) depicts, describes, or represents, in a manner patently offensive with respect to minors, an actual or simulated sexual act or sexual contact, an actual or simulated normal or perverted sexual act, or a lewd exhibition of the genitals or post-pubescent female breast; and

(C) taken as a whole, lacks serious literary, artistic, political, or scientific value for minors.

(7) Minor. The term "minor" means any person under 17 years of age.

History: (June 19, 1934, ch 652, Title II, Part I, § 231, as added Oct. 21, 1998, P.L. 105-277, Div C, Title XIV, § 1403, 112 Stat. 2681-736.)

HISTORY; ANCILLARY LAWS AND DIRECTIVES

Effective date of section:
This section took effect 30 days after enactment, pursuant to § 1406 of Title XIV of Div. C of Act Oct. 21, 1998, P.L. 105-277, which appears as 47 USCS § 223 note.

Other provisions:
Child Online Protection Act; congressional findings. Act Oct. 21, 1998, P.L. 105-277, Div. C, Title XIV, § 1402, 112 Stat. 2681-736, provides:
The Congress finds that—

(1) while custody, care, and nurture of the child resides first with the parent, the widespread availability of the Internet presents opportunities

for minors to access materials through the World Wide Web in a manner that can frustrate parental supervision or control;

(2) the protection of the physical and psychological well-being of minors by shielding them from materials that are harmful to them is a compelling governmental interest;

(3) to date, while the industry has developed innovative ways to help parents and educators restrict material that is harmful to minors through parental control protections and self-regulation, such efforts have not provided a national solution to the problem of minors accessing harmful material on the World Wide Web;

(4) a prohibition on the distribution of material harmful to minors, combined with legitimate defenses, is currently the most effective and least restrictive means by which to satisfy the compelling government interest; and

(5) notwithstanding the existence of protections that limit the distribution over the World Wide Web of material that is harmful to minors, parents, educators, and industry must continue efforts to find ways to protect children from being exposed to harmful material found on the Internet.

Study by Commission on Online Child Protection. Act Oct. 21, 1998, P.L. 105-277, Div C, Title XIV, § 1405, 112 Stat. 2681-739; Nov. 29, 1999, P.L. 106-113, Div B, § 1000(a)(9), 113 Stat. 1536 (enacting into law § 5001(b)–(f) of Subtitle H of Title IV of S. 1948 (113 Stat. 1501A-591), as introduced on Nov. 17, 1999); June 30, 2000, P.L. 106-229, Title IV, § 401, 114 Stat. 476, provides:

(a) Establishment. There is hereby established a temporary Commission to be known as the Commission on Online Child Protection (in this section referred to as the "Commission") for the purpose of conducting a study under this section regarding methods to help reduce access by minors to material that is harmful to minors on the Internet.

(b) Membership. The Commission shall be composed of 19 members, as follows:

(1) Industry members. The Commission shall include 16 members who shall consist of representatives of—

(A) providers of Internet filtering or blocking services or software;

(B) Internet access services;

(C) labeling or ratings services;

(D) Internet portal or search services;

(E) domain name registration services;

(F) academic experts; and

(G) providers that make content available over the Internet.

Of the members of the Commission by reason of this paragraph, an equal number shall be appointed by the Speaker of the House of Representatives and by the Majority Leader of the Senate. Members of the Commission appointed on or before October 31, 1999, shall remain members.

(2) Ex officio members. The Commission shall include the following officials:

(A) The Assistant Secretary (or the Assistant Secretary's designee).

(B) The Attorney General (or the Attorney General's designee).

(C) The Chairman of the Federal Trade Commission (or the Chairman's designee).

(3) Prohibition of pay. Members of the Commission shall not receive any pay by reason of their membership on the Commission.

(c) First Meeting. The Commission shall hold its first meeting not later than March 31, 2000.

(d) Chairperson. The chairperson of the Commission shall be elected by a vote of a majority of the members, which shall take place not later than 30 days after the first meeting of the Commission.

(e) Study.

(1) In general. The Commission shall conduct a study to identify technological or other methods that—

(A) will help reduce access by minors to material that is harmful to minors on the Internet; and

(B) may meet the requirements for use as affirmative defenses for purposes of section 231(c) of the Communications Act of 1934 [47 USCS § 231(c)] (as added by this title).

Any methods so identified shall be used as the basis for making legislative recommendations to the Congress under subsection (d)(3).

(2) Specific methods. In carrying out the study, the Commission shall identify and analyze various technological tools and methods for protecting minors from material that is harmful to minors, which shall include (without limitation)—

(A) a common resource for parents to use to help protect minors (such as a "one-click-away" resource);

(B) filtering or blocking software or services;

(C) labeling or rating systems;

(D) age verification systems;

(E) the establishment of a domain name for posting of any material that is harmful to minors; and

(F) any other existing or proposed technologies or methods for reducing access by minors to such material.

(3) Analysis. In analyzing technologies and other methods identified pursuant to paragraph (2), the Commission shall examine—

(A) the cost of such technologies and methods;

(B) the effects of such technologies and methods on law enforcement entities;

(C) the effects of such technologies and methods on privacy;

(D) the extent to which material that is harmful to minors is globally distributed and the effect of such technologies and methods on such distribution;

(E) the accessibility of such technologies and methods to parents; and

(F) such other factors and issues as the Commission considers relevant and appropriate.

(f) Report. Not later than 2 years after the enactment of this Act, the Commission shall submit a report to the Congress containing the results of the study under this section, which shall include—

(1) a description of the technologies and methods identified by the study and the results of the analysis of each such technology and method;

(2) the conclusions and recommendations of the Commission regarding each such technology or method;

(3) recommendations for legislative or administrative actions to implement the conclusions of the committee; and

(4) a description of the technologies or methods identified by the study that may meet the requirements for use as affirmative defenses for purposes of section 231(c) of the Communications Act of 1934 (as added by this title).

(g) Rules of the Commission.

(1) Quorum. Nine members of the Commission shall constitute a quorum for conducting the business of the Commission.

(2) Meetings. Any meetings held by the Commission shall be duly noticed at least 14 days in advance and shall be open to the public.

(3) Opportunities to testify. The Commission shall provide opportunities for representatives of the general public to testify.

(4) Additional rules. The Commission may adopt other rules as necessary to carry out this section.

(h) Gifts, bequests, and devises. The Commission may accept, use, and dispose of gifts, bequests, or devices of services or property, both real (including the use of office space) and personal, for the purpose of aiding or facilitating the work of the Commission. Gifts or grants not used at the termination of the Commission shall be returned to the donor or grantee.

(i)–(k) [not enacted]

(l) Termination. The Commission shall terminate 30 days after the submission of the report under subsection (d) or November 30, 2000, whichever occurs earlier.

(m) Inapplicability of Federal Advisory Committee Act. The Federal Advisory Committee Act (5 U.S.C. App.) shall not apply to the Commission.

First Amendment Timeline
Compiled by the Freedom Forum

Significant historical events, court cases, and ideas that have shaped our current system of constitutional First Amendment jurisprudence:

Pre–Nineteenth Century

1641

The Massachusetts General Court drafts the first broad statement of American liberties, the Massachusetts Body of Liberties. The document includes a right to petition and a statement about due process.

1663

Rhode Island grants religious freedom.

1689

Publication of John Locke's *Letter Concerning Toleration.* It provides the philosophical basis for George Mason's proposed Article XVI of the Virginia Declaration of Rights of 1776, which deals with religion. Mason's proposal provides that "all Men should enjoy the fullest toleration in the exercise of religion."

1708

Connecticut passes first dissenter statute and allows "full liberty of worship" to Anglicans and Baptists.

1735

Libel trial of New York publisher John Peter Zenger for published criticism of the royal governor of New York. Zenger is defended by Andrew Hamilton and acquitted. His trial establishes the principle that truth is a defense to libel and that a jury may determine whether a publication is defamatory or seditious.

1771

The State of Virginia jails fifty Baptist worshipers for preaching the Gospel contrary to the Anglican Book of Common Prayer.

1774

Eighteen Baptists are jailed in Massachusetts for refusing to pay taxes that support the Congregational Church.

1776

The Continental Congress adopts the final draft of the Declaration of Independence on July 4.

Virginia's House of Burgesses passes the Virginia Declaration of Rights. The Virginia Declaration is the first bill of rights to be included in a state constitution in America.

1777

Thomas Jefferson completes his first draft of a Virginia state bill for religious freedom, which states: "No man shall be forced to frequent or support any religious worship, place, or ministry whatsoever." The bill later becomes the famous Virginia Statute for Religious Freedom.

1786

The Virginia legislature adopts the Ordinance of Religious Freedom, which disestablishes the Anglican Church as the official church and prohibits harassment based on religious differences.

1787

Congress passes the Northwest Ordinance. Though primarily a law establishing government guidelines for colonization of new territory, it also provides that "religion, morality and knowledge being necessary also to good government and the happiness of mankind, schools and the means of education shall forever be encouraged."

1791

On December 15, Virginia becomes the eleventh state to approve the first ten amendments to the Constitution, the Bill of Rights.

1796

Andrew Jackson opposes the inclusion of the word "God" in Tennessee's Constitution.

1798

President John Adams oversees the passage of the Alien and Sedition Acts. In response, James Madison issues the "Virginia Resolution" and Thomas Jefferson introduces the "Kentucky Resolution" to give states the power to declare the Alien and Sedition Acts null and void.

On September 12, newspaper editor Benjamin Franklin Bache, the grandson of Benjamin Franklin, is arrested under the Sedition Act for libeling President John Adams.

The Nineteenth Century

The nineteenth century witnessed a Supreme Court hostile to many claims of freedom of speech and assembly. Fewer than twelve First Amendment cases came before the court between 1791 and 1889, according to First Amendment scholar Michael Gibson. This was due to the prevailing view among federal judges that the Bill of Rights did not apply to state actions.

1801

Congress lets the Sedition Act of 1798 expire, and President Thomas Jefferson pardons all persons convicted under the act. The act had punished those who uttered or published "false, scandalous, and malicious" writings against the government.

1836

The U.S. House of Representatives adopts gag rules preventing discussion of antislavery proposals. The House repeals the rules in 1844.

1859

John Stuart Mill publishes "On Liberty." The essay expands John Milton's argument that if speech is free and the search for knowledge unfettered, then eventually the truth will rise to the surface.

1863

General Ambrose Burnside of the Union Army orders the suspension of the publication of the *Chicago Times,* pursuant to the right of a commander to silence public expression of ideas and information deemed harmful to the military effort. Three days later, President Abraham Lincoln rescinds Burnside's order.

1864

General John A. Dix, a Union commander, orders the *New York Journal of Commerce* and the *New York World* closed after both papers publish a forged presidential proclamation purporting to order another draft of 400,000 men. Publication of the papers resumes two days later.

1868

The Fourteenth Amendment to the Constitution is ratified. The amendment, in part, requires that no state shall deprive "any person of life, liberty, or property, without due process of law; nor deny to any person within its jurisdiction the equal protection of the laws."

1891

The hundredth anniversary of the Bill of Rights is commemorated.

The Twentieth Century

Free-speech claims formed a substantive and integral part of the early-twentieth-century First Amendment cases that came before the U.S. Supreme Court, probably because of the extraordinary social upheavals of the era: massive late-nineteenth-century immigration movements, World War I, and the spread of socialism in the United States.

1907

In *Patterson v. Colorado*—its first free press case—the U.S. Supreme Court determines it does not have jurisdiction to review the "contempt" conviction of U.S. senator and Denver newspaper publisher Thomas Patterson for articles and a cartoon that criticized the state supreme court. The Court writes that "what constitutes contempt, as well as the time during which it may be committed, is a matter of local law." Leaving undecided the question of whether First Amendment guarantees are applicable to the states via the Fourteenth Amendment, the Court holds that free speech and free press guarantees guard only against prior restraint and do not prevent "subsequent punishment."

1917

Congress passes the Espionage Act, making it a crime "to willfully cause or attempt to cause insubordination, disloyalty, mutiny, or refusal of duty, in the military or naval forces of the United States," or to "willfully obstruct the recruiting or enlistment service" of the United States.

The Civil Liberties Bureau, a forerunner of the American Civil Liberties Union (ACLU), is formed to oppose the Espionage Act.

1918

Congress passes the Sedition Act, which forbids spoken or printed criticism of the U.S. government, the Constitution, or the flag.

1919

In *Schenck v. United States*, U.S. Supreme Court Justice Oliver Wendell Holmes sets forth his "clear and present danger" test: "whether the words used are used in such circumstances and are of such a nature as to create a clear and present danger that they will bring about the substantive evils that Congress has the right to prevent." Schenck and others were accused of urging draftees to oppose the draft and "not submit to intimidation." Justice Holmes also writes that not all speech is protected by the First Amendment, citing the now-famous example of falsely crying fire in a crowded theater.

In *Debs v. United States*, the U.S. Supreme Court upholds the conviction of socialist presidential candidate Eugene V. Debs under the Espionage Act for making speeches opposing World War I. Justice Holmes claims to apply the "clear and present danger" test, but he phrases it as requiring that Debs's words have a "natural tendency and reasonably probable effect" of obstructing recruitment.

1920

The American Civil Liberties Union (ACLU) is founded.

1921

Congress repeals the Sedition Act.

1925

In *Gitlow v. New York*, the U.S. Supreme Court upholds, under the New York criminal anarchy statute, Gitlow's conviction for writing and distributing *The Left Wing Manifesto*. The Court concludes, however, that the free speech clause of the First Amendment applies to the states through the due process clause of the Fourteenth Amendment.

The "Scopes Monkey Trial" occurs in Dayton, Tennessee. Schoolteacher John Thomas Scopes is found guilty of violating a Tennessee law that prohibits teaching the theory of evolution in public schools. The case pits famed orator William Jennings Bryan against famed defense attorney Clarence Darrow.

1926

H. L. Mencken is arrested for distributing copies of *American Mercury*. Censorship groups in Boston declare the periodical obscene.

1928

In *People of the State of New York ex rel. Bryant v. Zimmerman*, the U.S. Supreme Court upholds a New York law that mandates that organizations requiring their members to take oaths file certain organizational documents with the secretary of state. The Court writes: "There can be no doubt that under that power the state may prescribe and apply to associations having an oath-bound membership any reasonable regulation calculated to confine their purposes and activities within limits which are consistent with the rights of others and public welfare."

1931

In *Stromberg v. California*, the U.S. Supreme Court reverses the state court conviction of a nineteen-year-old female member of the Young Communist League, who violated a state law prohibiting the display of a red flag as "an emblem of opposition to the United States government." Legal commentators cite this case as the first in which the Court recognizes that protected speech may be nonverbal, or a form of symbolic expression.

In *Near v. Minnesota*, the U.S. Supreme Court invalidates a permanent injunction against the publisher of *The Saturday Press*. The Court rules that the Minnesota statute granting state judges the power to enjoin as a nuisance any "malicious, scandalous and defamatory newspaper, magazine or other periodical" is "the essence of censorship." The Court concluded that the primary aim of the First Amendment is to prevent prior restraints of the press.

1933

President Franklin D. Roosevelt pardons those convicted under the Espionage and Sedition Acts.

California repeals its Red Flag Law, which was ruled unconstitutional two years earlier in *Stromberg v. California*.

1936

In *Grosjean v. American Press Co.*, the U.S. Supreme Court invalidates a state tax on newspaper advertising that is applied to papers with a circulation exceeding 20,000 copies per week as a violation of the First Amendment. The Court finds the tax unconstitutional because "it is seen to be a deliberate and calculated device in the guise of a tax to limit the circulation of information to which the public is entitled."

1937

In *DeJonge v. Oregon*, the U.S. Supreme Court reverses the conviction of an individual, under a state criminal syndicalism law, for participation in a Communist Party political meeting. The Court writes that "peaceable assembly for lawful discussion cannot be made a crime. The holding of meetings for peaceable political action cannot be proscribed."

1938

Life magazine is banned in the United States for publishing pictures from the public health film *The Birth of a Baby*.

1939

Georgia, Massachusetts, and Connecticut finally ratify the Bill of Rights.

1940

Congress passes the Smith Act, or the Alien Registration Act of 1940, which makes it a crime to advocate the violent overthrow of the government.

In *Thornhill v. Alabama*, the U.S. Supreme Court strikes down an Alabama law prohibiting loitering and picketing "without a just cause or legal excuse" near businesses. The Court writes: "The freedom of speech and of the press guaranteed by the Constitution embraces at the least the liberty to discuss publicly and truthfully all matters of public concern without previous restraint or fear of subsequent punishment."

In *Cantwell v. Connecticut*, the U.S. Supreme Court holds for the first time that the due process clause of the Fourteenth Amendment makes the free exercise clause of the First Amendment applicable to states.

1941

Congress authorizes President Franklin D. Roosevelt to create the Office of Censorship.

1942

The U.S. Supreme Court determines that "fighting words" are not protected by the First Amendment. In *Chaplinsky v. New Hampshire*, the Court defines "fighting words" as "those which by their very utterance inflict injury or tend to incite an immediate breach of peace." The Court states that such words are "no essential part of any exposition of ideas, and are of such slight social value as a step to truth that any benefit that may be derived from them is clearly outweighed by the social interest in order and morality."

1943

In *West Virginia State Board of Education v. Barnette*, the U.S. Supreme Court rules that a West Virginia requirement to salute the flag violates the free speech clause of the First Amendment.

In *National Broadcasting Co. v. United States*, the U.S. Supreme Court states that no one has a First Amendment right to a radio license or to monopolize a radio frequency.

1947

In *Everson v. Board of Education*, the U.S. Supreme Court upholds a state program that reimburses parents for money spent on transporting their children to parochial schools. The Court finds that the state provision of free bus transportation to all school children amounts only to a general service benefit and safeguards children rather than aiding religion.

1949

In *Terminiello v. Chicago*, the U.S. Supreme Court limits the scope of the "fighting words" doctrine. Writing for the majority, Justice William O. Douglas says that the "function of free speech . . . is to invite dispute. It may indeed best serve its high purpose when it induces a condition of unrest, creates dissatisfaction with conditions as they are, or even stirs people to anger."

1951

In *Dennis v. United States*, the U.S. Supreme Court upholds the convictions of twelve Communist Party members who were convicted under the Smith Act of 1940. The Court finds that the Smith Act, a measure banning speech that advocates the violent overthrow of the federal government, is not in undue conflict with the First Amendment.

1957

The U.S. Supreme Court determines that "obscenity is not within the area of constitutionally protected speech or press." In *Roth v. United States*, the Court defines obscenity as "material which deals with sex in a manner appealing to prurient interest." The mere portrayal of sex, however, in art, literature, scientific works, and similar forums "is not itself sufficient reason to deny material the constitutional protection of freedom of speech and press," the Court states. Additionally, the Court notes that speech is obscene when "to the average person applying contemporary community standards, the dominant theme of the material taken as a whole appeals to prurient interests."

1958

The U.S. Supreme Court allows the National Association for the Advancement of Colored People (NAACP) of Alabama to withhold its membership list from Alabama lawmakers. In *NAACP v. Alabama*, the Court states that the demand by Alabama officials for the NAACP to provide them a membership list violates members' associational rights.

1959

The U.S. Supreme Court upholds the conviction of a college professor who refuses, on First Amendment grounds, to answer questions before the House Un-American Activities Committee. In *Barenblatt v. United States*, the Court states that, where "First Amendment rights are asserted to bar governmental interrogation, resolution of the issue always involves a balancing by the courts of the competing private and public interests at stake." The Court concludes that the investigation is for a valid legislative purpose and that "investigatory power in this domain is not to be denied Congress solely because the field of education is involved."

1962

The U.S. Supreme Court rules that a state-composed, nondenominational prayer violates the Establishment Clause of the First Amendment. In *Engel v. Vitale*, the Court states that such a prayer represents government sponsorship of religion.

1963

The U.S. Supreme Court finds that a South Carolina policy denying unemployment compensation to a Seventh Day Adventist who refused to work on Saturdays is in violation of the Free Exercise Clause of the First Amendment. In *Sherbert v. Verner*, the Court determines that a law that has the unintended effect of burdening religious beliefs will be upheld only when it is the least restrictive means of accomplishing a compelling state objective.

1964

In *New York Times v. Sullivan*, the U.S. Supreme Court overturns a libel judgment against the *New York Times*. The Court rules that public officials may not recover damages for a defamatory falsehood relating to their conduct unless they prove the statement was made with actual malice. The Court defines "actual malice" as "with knowledge that it was false or with reckless disregard of whether it was false or not."

1966

The U.S. Supreme Court invalidates a Massachusetts court decision that found the 1750 book *A Woman of Pleasure* obscene. In *Memoirs v. Massachusetts*, Justice William Brennan writes that a book that possesses the requisite prurient appeal to be declared obscene cannot be banned unless it is found to be utterly without redeeming social value.

In *Elfbrant v. Russell*, the U.S. Supreme Court invalidates an Arizona statute requiring the dismissal of any state employee who knowingly becomes a member of the Communist Party or any party whose intentions include overthrowing the U.S. government.

In *Sheppard v. Maxwell*, the U.S. Supreme Court reverses the murder conviction of Dr. Sam Sheppard because the trial judge failed to quell publicity surrounding the trial.

1967

In *United States v. O'Brien*, the U.S. Supreme Court upholds the conviction of David Paul O'Brien, an antiwar protester accused of violating a federal statute prohibiting the public destruction of draft cards. O'Brien claims that the burning of draft cards is "symbolic speech" protected by the First Amendment. The Court concludes that conduct combining "speech" and "nonspeech" elements can be regulated if the following four requirements are met: (1) the regulation is within the constitutional power of the government; (2) it furthers an "important or substantial" government interest; (3) the interest is "unrelated to suppression of free expression"; and (4) "incidental restriction" of First Amendment freedoms is "no greater than is essential to the furtherance" of the government interest. The Court concludes that all requirements were satisfied in this case.

1968

In *Epperson v. Arkansas*, the U.S. Supreme Court invalidates an Arkansas statute prohibiting public schoolteachers from teaching evolution. The Court finds that the statute violates the establishment clause because it bans the teaching of evolution solely on religious grounds.

1969

The U.S. Supreme Court vindicates the rights of public school students who were suspended for wearing black armbands to school in protest of the Vietnam War. In *Tinker v. Des Moines Independent School District*, the Court rules that the prohibition violates the students' First Amendment rights. Justice Abe Fortas writes that students do not "shed their constitutional rights to freedom of speech or expression at the schoolhouse gate."

In *Brandenburg v. Ohio*, the U.S. Supreme Court rules that speech advocating the use of force or crime is not protected if (1) the advocacy is "directed to inciting or producing imminent lawless action" and (2) the advocacy is also "likely to incite or produce such action."

In *Stanley v. Georgia*, the U.S. Supreme Court rules that the First and Fourteenth Amendments protect a person's "private possession of obscene matter" from criminal prosecution. The Court notes that the state, although possessing broad authority to regulate obscene material, cannot punish private possession of such in an individual's own home.

In *Red Lion Broadcasting Co. v. Federal Communication Commission*, the U.S. Supreme Court finds that Congress and the FCC did not violate the First Amendment when they required a radio or television station to allow response time to persons subjected to personal attacks and political editorializing on air.

1970

In *Walz v. Tax Commission*, the U.S. Supreme Court finds that a state law exempting from taxation the property or income of religious organizations does not violate the Establishment Clause. The Court states that history has revealed no danger that such exemptions will give rise to either a religious effect or an entanglement of government and religion.

1971

In *New York Times v. United States*, the U.S. Supreme Court allows continued publication of the Pentagon Papers. The Court holds that the central purpose of the First Amendment is to "prohibit the widespread practice of governmental suppression of embarrassing information." This case establishes that the press has almost absolute immunity from prepublication restraints.

In *Cohen v. California*, the U.S. Supreme Court reverses the breach-of-peace conviction of an individual who wore a jacket with the words "F—— the Draft" into a courthouse. The Court concludes that offensive and profane speech are protected by the First Amendment.

In *Lemon v. Kurtzman*, the U.S. Supreme Court establishes a three-part test to determine whether a governmental action violates the Establishment Clause. The test specifies that (1) the action must have a secular purpose; (2) its primary effect must neither advance nor inhibit religion; and (3) there must be no excessive government entanglement.

1972

In *Branzburg v. Hayes*, the U.S. Supreme Court rules that the First Amendment does not exempt reporters from "performing the citizen's normal duty of appearing and furnishing information relevant to the grand jury's task." The Court rejects a reporter's claim that the flow of information available to the press will be seriously curtailed if reporters are forced to release the names of confidential sources for use in a government investigation.

In *Wisconsin v. Yoder*, the U.S. Supreme Court rules that the State of Wisconsin cannot require Amish children to attend school beyond the eighth grade.

In *Lloyd Corp. v. Tanner*, the U.S. Supreme Court rules that owners of a shopping center may bar antiwar activists from distributing leaflets at the center. The Court finds that citizens do not have a First Amendment right to express themsleves on privately owned property.

1973

In *Miller v. California*, the U.S. Supreme Court defines the test for determining if speech is obscene: (1) whether the "average person applying contemporary community standards" would find that the work, taken as a whole, appeals to the prurient interest; (2) whether the work depicts or describes, in a patently offensive way, sexual conduct specifically defined by the applicable state law; and (3) whether the work, taken as a whole, lacks serious literary, artistic, political or scientific value.

In *Paris Adult Theatre I v. Slaton*, the U.S. Supreme Court rules that a state may constitutionally prohibit exhibitions or displays of obscenity, even if access to the exhibitions is limited to consenting adults.

1974

In *Miami Herald Publishing Co. v. Tornillo*, the U.S. Supreme Court invalidates a state law requiring newspapers to give free reply space to political candidates the newspapers criticize. The Court rules that the right of newspaper editors to choose what they wish to print or not to print cannot be infringed to allow public access to the print media.

1976

In *Buckley v. Valeo*, the U.S. Supreme Court rules that certain provisions of the Federal Election Campaign Act of 1976, which limits expenditures to political campaigns, violate the First Amendment.

The U.S. Supreme Court rules that the First Amendment does not apply to privately owned shopping centers. In *Hudgens v. National Labor Relations Board*, the Court holds that as long as the state does not encourage, aid, or command the suppression of free speech, the First Amendment is not subverted by the actions of shopping center owners.

The U.S. Supreme Court finds that an appropriately defined zoning ordinance barring the location of an "adult movie theatre" within a hundred feet of any two other "regulated uses" does not violate the First Amendment—even if the theater is not showing obscene material. In *Young v. American Mini Theaters*, the Court concludes that the ordinance is not a prior restraint and is a proper use of the city's zoning authority.

The U.S. Supreme Court rules that the public has a First Amendment right to the free flow of truthful information about lawful commercial activities. In *Virginia State Board of Pharmacy v. Virginia Citizens Consumer Council*, the Court invalidates a Virginia law prohibiting the advertisement of prescription drug prices.

1977

In *Abood v. Detroit Board of Education*, the U.S. Supreme Court declares that a state may require a public employee to pay dues to organizations such as unions and state bars, as long as the money is used for purposes such as collective bargaining and contract and grievance hearings. The Court notes that, pursuant to the First Amendment, state workers may not be forced to give to political candidates or to fund political messages unrelated to their employee organization's bargaining function.

1978

In *NSPA v. Skokie*, the Illinois Supreme Court rules that the National Socialist Party of America (NSPA), a neo-Nazi group, can march through Skokie, Illinois, a community inhabited by a number of Holocaust survivors.

The U.S. Supreme Court upholds the power of the FCC to regulate indecent speech broadcast over the air. In *FCC v. Pacifica*, the Court allows FCC regulation because the broadcast media are a "uniquely pervasive presence" and easily accessible to children. The Court, however, does make clear that, although the government can constitutionally regulate indecent speech in the broadcast media, it does not have power to enforce a total ban on such speech.

1980

In *Central Hudson Gas & Electric Corporation v. Public Service Commission*, the U.S. Supreme Court sets forth a four-part test for determining when commercial speech may or may not be regulated by states. The test states that: (1) the commercial speech must not be misleading or involve illegal activity; (2) the government interest that is advanced by the regulation must be substantial; (3) the regulation must directly advance the asserted government interest; and (4) the government regulation must not be more extensive than is necessary to serve the governmental interest at stake.

1982

In *Board of Education v. Pico*, the U.S. Supreme Court rules that school officials may not remove books from school libraries because they disagree with the ideas contained in the books.

1984

Congress passes the Equal Access Act. This federal law prohibits secondary schools that are receiving federal financial assistance from denying equal access to student groups on the basis of religious, political, or philosophical beliefs or because of the content of their speech.

1985

In *Wallace v. Jaffree*, the U.S. Supreme Court invalidates an Alabama law authorizing a one-minute silent period at the start of each school day "for meditation or voluntary prayer." The Court finds that the law was enacted to endorse religion, thus violating the Establishment Clause.

1986

In *Witters v. Washington Department of Services for the Blind*, the U.S. Supreme Court rules that a vocational rehabilitation-assistance program that awards grants and scholarships to students does not violate the Establishment Clause, even if some recipients use the funds to attend religious schools.

1987

In *Edwards v. Aquillard*, the U.S. Supreme Court invalidates a Louisiana statute that bars the teaching of evolution in public schools unless the teaching is accompanied by instruction about creationism.

1988

In *Hazelwood School District v. Kuhlmeier*, the U.S. Supreme Court rules that school officials may exercise editorial control over content of school-sponsored student publications if they do so in a way that is reasonably related to legitimate pedagogical concerns.

1989

Congress passes the Flag Protection Act, which punishes anyone who "knowingly mutilates, defaces, physically defiles, burns, maintains on the floor or ground, or tramples upon any U.S. flag."

In *Texas v. Johnson*, the U.S. Supreme Court rules that burning the American flag is a constitutionally protected form of free speech.

1990

In *United States v. Eichman*, the U.S. Supreme Court invalidates the Flag Protection Act of 1989. The Court finds that the statute violates free speech.

In *Board of Education of Westside Community Schools v. Mergens*, the U.S. Supreme Court finds the Equal Access Act constitutional.

In *Employment Division v. Smith*, the U.S. Supreme Court rules that "the right of free exercise does not relieve an individual of the obligation to comply with a valid and neutral law of general applicability on the ground that the law proscribes . . . conduct that his religion prescribes."

1991

In *Simon & Schuster v. Members of the New York State Crime Victims Board*, the U.S. Supreme Court invalidates the New York "Son of Sam" law that requires convicted persons to turn over to the state proceeds from any work describing their crimes. Justice Sandra Day O'Connor finds that the law is overbroad and that it regulates speech based on content.

The bicentennial anniversary of the ratification of the Bill of Rights is commemorated.

1992

In *Lee v. Weisman*, the U.S. Supreme Court determines that an administrative policy allowing religious invocations at public high school graduation ceremonies violates the Establishment Clause.

In *R.A.V. v. City of St. Paul*, the U.S. Supreme Court invalidates a Minnesota hate speech statute, saying it violates the First Amendment.

1993

In *Zobrest v. Catalina Foothills School District*, the U.S. Supreme Court finds that the Establishment Clause is not subverted when a public school district provides a sign-language interpreter to a deaf student attending a parochial school within the district's boundaries. The Court states that it has "consistently held that government programs that neutrally provide benefits to a broad class of citizens defined without reference to religion are not readily subject to an Establishment Clause challenge because sectarian institutions may also receive an attenuated financial benefit."

Congress passes the Religious Freedom Restoration Act.

1994

In *Board of Education of Kiryas Joel Village School District v. Grumet*, the U.S. Supreme Court rules that a 1989 New York law creating a separate school district for a small religious village violates the Establishment Clause.

In *Rosenberger v. Rectors of the University of Virginia*, the U.S. Supreme Court invalidates a policy denying funds to a Christian student newspaper on free speech and Establishment Clause grounds. The Court finds that once a public university chooses to fund some student viewpoints, it may not choose which viewpoints to fund.

1996

In *44 Liquormart v. State of Rhode Island*, the U.S. Supreme Court invalidates a state law forbidding all advertising of liquor prices.

1997

In *Reno II v. ACLU*, the U.S. Supreme Court rules that the federal Communications Decency Act of 1996 is unconstitutional. The Court concludes that the act, which makes it a crime to put adult-oriented material on the Internet where a child may find it, is too vague and tramples on the free speech rights of adults.

In *Boerne v. Flores*, the U.S. Supreme Court finds that the 1993 Religious Freedom Restoration Act is unconstitutional.

1998

Congress enacts the Child Online Protection Act (COPA), which attaches federal criminal liability to the online transmission for commercial purposes of material considered harmful to minors. Challengers attack the law on First Amendment grounds, and a federal appeals court upholds a lower court injunction against enforcement of COPA in June 1999.

In *National Endowment for the Arts v. Finley*, the U.S. Supreme Court rules that a federal statute requiring the NEA to consider general standards of decency before awarding grant monies to artists does not infringe on First Amendment rights.

In *Arkansas Educational Television Commission v. Forbes*, the U.S. Supreme Court holds that a public television station may exclude a legally qualified candidate from participating in a station-sponsored debate if the station concludes that the excluded individual is not a politically viable candidate. The Court declares the station-sponsored debate to be a nonpublic forum, ruling that exclusion of the candidate for reasonable and viewpoint-neutral reasons is allowed.

President Bill Clinton revises his 1995 "Guidelines on Religious Expression in Public Schools" in an effort to promote public understanding of the fact that the First Amendment provides for religious expression by students while simultaneously forbidding government-sponsored religion. The 1998 revised guidelines are mailed to every school superintendent in the country.

1999

In *Wilson v. Layne* and *Hanlon v. Berger*, the U.S. Supreme Court rules unanimously that law enforcement officials violate privacy rights protected by the Fourth Amendment when they allow media on ride-alongs into a home when making an arrest or conducting a search. Though the consolidated cases more squarely address Fourth Amendment issues, the newsgathering technique of "ride-along" is at the heart of the dispute.

The U.S. Court of Appeals for the Fourth Circuit hears *Food Lion v. Capital Cities/ABC, Inc.*, in which the press is found liable for information gathered in an undercover investigation; Food Lion does not question the veracity of the information but rather the newsgathering methods used to obtain it. The Fourth Circuit characterizes Food Lion's attempt to claim millions of dollars in punitive damages without proving the falsity of the news report as an unacceptable "end-run around First Amendment strictures" and reduces the damages awarded by the jury to a mere two dollars.

President Clinton orders the Department of Education to mail guidelines on religious liberty to all public schools. The mass mailing emphasizes once again the administration's commitment to providing schools with guidance about the proper role of religion in the schools under current law.

2000

In *Boy Scouts of America v. Dale*, the U.S. Supreme Court rules that application of a public accommodation law to force the Boy Scouts to accept a gay scoutmaster is a violation of the private organization's freedom of association guaranteed by the First Amendment.

In *Mitchell v. Helms*, the U.S. Supreme Court finds that a federal program allowing states to lend educational material and equipment to both public and private schools does not violate the Establishment Clause of the First Amendment.

In *Santa Fe Independent School District v. Doe*, the U.S. Supreme Court rules that a school district's policy permitting student-led, student-initiated prayer at football games violates the Establishment Clause of the First Amendment.

Consumers Union, Filtering Software Test:
Digital Chaperones for Kids

© Consumers Union of the United States, Inc.

Which Internet filters protect the best?
Which get in the way?

Are you concerned that your kids will encounter sexually explicit material on-line? Recent studies show that such content appears on just 2 percent of Web sites. Even so, it's easy to reach a site with X-rated content, via a major search engine, using terms like "Bambi" or "adult." If you use a more suggestive word for the search, you will be steered to hundreds of sexually oriented sites. Pornography isn't the only troublesome area. According to the Simon Wiesenthal Center, there are now some three thousand hate-promoting Web sites. Countless other sites accessible to children promote drug use, fraud, or bomb making.

The federal government hasn't been effective at restricting children's access to sexually oriented content online. The Supreme Court struck down one law, the Communications Decency Act, on First Amendment grounds. In December Congress passed the Children's Internet Protection Act. This legislation would require schools and libraries that want federal funding to filter objectionable Internet content.

The only federal law offering explicit protection to young Web surfers at home is the Child Online Privacy Protection Act, which prohibits any Web site from collecting a child's personal information without parental consent.

Who has the primary responsibility for protecting children when they go online at home? The parents of the 26 million American youngsters who surf the Web, that's who.

According to a recent survey by Jupiter Research, seven out of ten parents handle the issue by being present when their kids go online. Only 6 percent

This article originally appeared in 66:3 *Consumer Reports* 20 (March 2001).

use stand-alone filtering software, products that promise to steer kids clear of undesirable material.

Does that small minority know something? Can a technological fix substitute for a parent's watchful eye? In 1997, when we first tested this kind of software, the answer clearly was no. But since then, the number of software filters has grown from a handful to well over a dozen. Internet giant America Online (AOL) comes with parental controls that filter content.

Is the present generation of filtering software any better than its predecessors? To find out, we bought nine of the most widely used titles, ranging in price from $39 to $80. Most are written only for Windows computers, not Macintoshes. We also tested AOL's parental controls.

Some filters proved to be so simplistic or so complex to set up effectively that we didn't test them fully. And a few dropped off the market while our tests were under way. In the end, we rated six products plus AOL's parental controls.

THE BASICS OF FILTERING

Each product we tested filters Web content by interposing itself between your computer's Web browser and Internet connection, then preventing objectionable content from getting through. Some let you decide in advance whether to filter different types of content, such as profanity or sex information. Depending on the product and how a user configures it, a child trying to access an off-limits site may receive a warning message, a browser error message, or a partial view of the blocked site. Sometimes the browser itself will shut down.

Filtering-software designers use one of three approaches to determining whether a site merits blocking:

- Software analysis. A site's contents can be rapidly analyzed by software. The filter may render a judgment at the time a child tries to access a site, or check a list of sites to block. The presence of certain phrases or images may render the site objectionable.

   While efficient, software analysis has its drawbacks. The software may decide to block a Web site that's completely above reproach only because it contains a prohibited word. It may partially block a site, preventing text from appearing but letting through photos or onscreen images with embedded text. Or it may block images but not text. Most software we tested blocked both words and images.

   For example, in 1999 Dr. Jamie McKenzie, publisher of an online journal about educational technology, found his site blocked by a major filtering product, which warned users that McKenzie's site was in the "sexually explicit" category because it contained a file named adult.html. The blocking was lifted after McKenzie complained.

• Human analysis. Some companies have their staff review sites individually, then place them on a list to be blocked or designated as suitable for children.

This time-consuming process limits the number of sites that can be reviewed. Given the Web's volatility, chances are that numerous objectionable sites will remain perpetually outside the reviewers' scrutiny.

• Site labeling. Several of the products we tested incorporate a popular ratings system run by the nonprofit Internet Content Ratings Association (ICRA). This program, in which Web site owners voluntarily label their content, has been around for several years. The ICRA system recently expanded its labeling to include drugs, alcohol, tobacco, and weapons, plus the context in which words appear.

Microsoft's Internet Explorer browser can filter sites using these labels, including the expanded ICRA labeling. (You'll find it listed as "content advisor" under Internet Options in the Explorer menu.) Netscape's browser doesn't have the feature.

We found this feature in Explorer ineffective as the sole filtering technique, because the many sexually explicit sites that aren't rated won't be blocked. You can set the feature to block all unrated sites. But that will block so many unrated conventional sites—including, for example, the White House, the U.S. Senate, the House of Representatives, and the Supreme Court—that it makes browsing pointless.

Site labeling also depends on the honesty with which sites rate themselves. We found one site containing profanity that slipped past Explorer's filter because the site owner chose a label that didn't accurately reflect the site's content. Until far more sites suitable for children are properly labeled, labeling must be considered a complement to other filtering techniques, rather like motion picture ratings.

HOW WELL DO FILTERS BLOCK BAD STUFF?

Our main test determined how well the filters blocked objectionable content. We configured all six products for a 13-to-15-year-old; we also tested AOL's Young Teen (ages 13 to 15) and Mature Teen (ages 16 to 17) parental controls. We pitted them all against a list of 86 easily located Web sites that contain sexually explicit content or violently graphic images, or that promote drugs, tobacco, crime, or bigotry.

AOL's Young Teen control, the best by far, allowed only one site through in its entirety, along with portions of about 20 other sites. All the other filters allowed at least 20 percent of the sites through in their entirety. Net Nanny displayed parts of more than a dozen sites, often with forbidden words expunged but graphic images intact.

Why did Young Teen perform so well? According to AOL, the Young Teen control lets kids see only the sites on its approved list, while Mature Teen blocks access to a list of prohibited sites. Kids could view an inappropriate site just because it wasn't on the Mature Teen list. (AOL considers the lists proprietary and does not disclose the number of sites on them.)

Only a few filters were able to block certain inappropriate sites. In some cases, that probably reflected differences in filtering techniques more than differences in judgment. Faulty though it may be, for example, filtering based on objectionable words apparently helped Net Nanny and Internet Guard Dog intercept a site with instructions on bomb making that eluded most others.

However, differences in judgment seem the most likely explanation for why only Cyber Patrol and both AOL controls blocked the Operation Rescue anti-abortion Web site, which contains photos of aborted fetuses. Such differences raise questions about how people decide what gets blocked.

DO FILTERS BLOCK GOOD STUFF?

In some cases, filters block harmless sites merely because their software does not consider the context in which a word or phrase is used. Far more troubling is when a filter appears to block legitimate sites based on moral or political value judgments.

Prominent filters like Cyber Patrol and Cybersitter 2000 may make some people suspect that value judgments come into play because their makers refuse to divulge the blocked-site lists. Last October the Library of Congress ruled that such lists could be made public by anyone who could decipher the data files in which they are stored.

To see whether the filters interfere with legitimate content, we pitted them against a list of 53 Web sites that featured serious content on controversial subjects.

Results varied widely. While most blocked only a few sites, Cybersitter 2000 and Internet Guard Dog blocked nearly one in five. AOL's Young Teen control blocked 63 percent of the sites. According to AOL, its staff and subscriber parents choose the sites kids are allowed to see using the control, with an emphasis on educational and entertainment sites. Our test sites may have been blocked because they didn't meet AOL's criteria, not because they were controversial.

Our results cast doubt on the appropriateness of some companies' judgments. Perhaps the most extreme example of conflicting judgments: the ones applied to the site of Peacefire, an antifiltering site that provides instructions on how to bypass filtering products. AOL, Cyber Patrol, and Cybersitter 2000, which keep their blocked-site lists secret, blocked Peacefire. Net Nanny, which makes its list public, didn't block it.

RECOMMENDATIONS

Filtering software is no substitute for parental supervision. Most of the products we tested failed to block one objectionable site in five. America Online's Young Teen (or Kids Only) setting provides the best protection, though it will likely curb access to Web sites addressing political and social issues.

If you're not an AOL user but still want some restriction on your kids' access to the Internet, consider which product's features best suit your needs. Some examples:

- Cyber Patrol, the most full-featured product, has the most extensive controls over when your child can go online, plus the ability to block or unblock sites that deal with sex education.
- Cybersitter 2000 and Norton Internet Security 2001 both let you control access to at least 20 categories of subject matter.
- Cybersitter 2000, Net Nanny, and Cyber Snoop can all keep a log of your child's online activity, including any attempts to view blocked sites.

Nearly all the filters offer some control over the disclosure of personal information, such as name and address. But we found such privacy protection too weak to rely on.

People who visit sites they don't want their kids to see can delete the browser's off-line files—where it saves copies of recently visited Web pages. And you can check your child's recent online activities by reviewing the browser's history list and bookmarks. To check for any adult images your child may have downloaded from the Internet, search your hard drive for recent files with names ending in .gif, .jpg, .tif, or .zip.

Two sites that provide information on how to protect children online are www.getnetwise.org and www.safekids.com.

RATINGS: FILTERING SOFTWARE

Filtering software is a basic software filter that purports to prevent children from reaching inappropriate Web sites. Some products add antivirus protection or rudimentary privacy safeguards. America Online includes a "parental controls" filter in its service. Otherwise, filtering software is a product you buy at retail or download.

The judgments below tell you how well the tested products blocked inappropriate content (typically preventing both words and images from appearing onscreen) and did not block legitimate content, and how easy the filters were to use. The bottom line: Don't expect miracles.

Protection is a filter's ability to block Web sites containing objectionable material, such as sexual content or promotion of crime, bigotry, violence, tobacco, or drugs. Failure to block at least 35 percent of these sites was judged poor. Partial blockage of a site (showing images but no words, or vice versa) was considered less effective than total blockage. *Interference* is how often a filter blocked Web sites containing potentially controversial but legitimate material, such as sex education, the abortion rights debate, or gun control. *Features* is the number of features related to filtering and child protection. *Price* is the estimated national average. The numbers indicate the following scale of ratings: 5—excellent; 4—very good; 3—good; 2—fair; 1—poor.

Online Service
America Online Parental Controls
Part of AOL service, which costs $21.95 per month.
www.aol.com

Young Teen (ages 13–15)
Protection: 4
Interference: 1
Features: 3

Mature Teen (ages 16-17)
Protection: 2
Interference: 4
Features: 3

Young Teen is pretty effective, though it will block many legitimate sites. Mature Teen isn't suitable for unattended Web filtering. Young Teen failed to block 14 percent of objectionable sites; Mature Teen, 30 percent. Filtering is hard to defeat because it's handled through AOL's centralized service. For some objectionable sites, both controls blocked images but not text. Young Teen blocked 63 percent of legitimate sites. Neither control can block personal information entered into Web sites.

Features: Online list of objectionable Web sites, automatically updated. Can limit total hours of Web access, filter mail. Can also be set for highly restricted Kids Only mode, for ages 12 and under. Available for both Windows and Macintosh.

Stand-Alone Software
All products filter personal information entered into Web sites and filter use of chat rooms. Except as noted, these run only on Windows computers, let you limit time spent on the Web, and can be configured for multiple users. Products are listed alphabetically.

Cyber Patrol, version 4
Surf Control Inc.
www.cyberpatrol.com

> Protection: 3
> Interference: 5
> Features: 5

So-so Web blocking; most useful for restricting the time online to certain days and hours or limiting the total number of hours a child can be online. Failed to block 23 percent of objectionable sites. Feature to protect personal information can be defeated very simply. Can filter mail, sites labeled with content ratings. Blocks selected applications (such as personal-finance or scheduling programs), not just the browser. Online list of objectionable Web sites, automatically updated. The only stand-alone software tested that has a Macintosh version. Costs $50. Costs $30/year for site-list updates.

Cybersitter 2000
Solid Oak Software Inc.
www.cybersitter.com

Protection: 3
Interference: 3
Features: 4

So-so Web blocking; most useful for tracking kids' activity. Failed to block 22 percent of objectionable sites. Can't be configured for multiple users. Online list of objectionable Web sites, automatically updated. Can filter mail, downloads, custom word list. Can select subjects to block from detailed list. Can log activity. Costs $40.

Cyber Snoop
Pearl Software, Inc.
www.pearlsw.com

Protection: 1
Interference: 5
Features: 4

Not suitable for unattended Web filtering. Failed to block 90 percent of objectionable sites. Relies on parents entering lists of objectionable or permissible Web sites; changing user requires restarting Windows. Can filter mail, downloads, sites labeled with some content ratings, custom word list. Can log activity. Costs $50.

Internet Guard Dog
McAfee Software Division of Network Associates, Inc.
www.mcafee.com

Protection: 2
Interference: 3
Features: 2

Not suitable for unattended Web filtering; most useful for blocking ads and cookies. Failed to block 30 percent of objectionable sites. Can't filter newsgroups. Relies on parents entering lists of objectionable or permissible Web sites. Can filter sites labeled with content ratings, custom word list. Can block ads, filter cookies, automatically clear Web "history" list from browser. Costs $39.

Net Nanny, version 4
Net Nanny Ltd.
www.netnanny.com

> Protection: 1
> Interference: 4
> Features: 4

Not suitable for unattended Web filtering. Failed to block 52 percent of objectionable sites, in numerous cases blocking words but not images. List of objectionable Web sites, automatically updated. Filters custom word list, sites labeled with some content ratings. Can log activity. Costs $50.

Norton Internet Security 2001 Family Edition
Symantec Corp.
www.symantec.com

> Protection: 3
> Interference: 4
> Protection: 4

So-so Web filtering; most useful as firewall, antivirus protection, and ad blocker. Failed to block 20 percent of objectionable sites. Can't limit time of Web access. Online list of objectionable Web sites, automatically updated. Can filter mail, downloads. Can select subjects to block from detailed list. Blocks selected applications that access the Internet, not just the browser. Can block ads, screen viruses ($4/year subscription), act as personal firewall against computer hackers. Costs $80; $11/year for site-list updates; telephone support costs $30 per problem.

RESOURCES

Organizations That Support Internet Restrictions

American Center for Law and Justice, P.O. Box 64429, Virginia Beach, VA 23467; (757) 226-2489; www.aclj.org.

American Family Association, P.O. Box 2440, Tupelo, MS 38803; (662) 844-5036; www.afa.net.

Enough Is Enough, P.O. Box 26228, Santa Ana, CA 92799-6228; (714) 435-9056 or (888) 236-6844; www.enough.org.

Family Research Council, 801 G Street, N.W., Washington, DC 20001; (202) 393-2100; www.frc.org.

National Coalition for the Protection of Children and Families, 800 Compton Road, Suite 9224, Cincinnati, OH 45231; (513) 521-6227; www.nationalcoalition.org.

National Law Center for Families and Children, 3819 Plaza Drive, Fairfax, VA 22030-2512; (703) 691-4626; www.nationallawcenter.org.

Organizations That Oppose Internet Restrictions

American Civil Liberties Union, Cyber-Liberties, 125 Broad Street, 18th Floor, New York, NY 10004-2400; (212) 549-2500; www.aclu.org/issues/cyber/hmcl.html.

American Library Association, Office for Intellectual Freedom, 50 E. Huron, Chicago, IL 60611; (800) 545-2433; www.ala.org.

Center for Democracy and Technology, 1634 Eye Street N.W., Suite 1100, Washington, DC 20006; (202) 637-9800; www.cdt.org.

Electronic Frontier Foundation, 1550 Bryant Street, Suite 725, San Francisco, CA 94103; (415) 436-9333; www.eff.org.

Electronic Privacy Information Center, 1718 Connecticut Avenue, N.W.,
   Suite 200, Washington, DC 20009; (202) 483-1140; www.epic.org.
People for the American Way, 2000 M Street, N.W., Suite 400, Washington,
   DC 20036; (202) 467-4999 or (800) 326-7329; www.pfaw.org.

General Sources of Information About Cyberlaw

Cyberspace Law Center, cyber.findlaw.com, is a resource for those interested
   in legal issues concerning cyberspace. It is maintained by Findlaw, a com-
   prehensive searchable legal index, and LawCrawler, which searches legal
   sites throughout the Internet.
The UCLA Online Institute for Cyberspace Law and Policy, www.gseis.
   ucla.edu/iclp/hp.html, provides an overview of recent books and journal
   articles, including a growing number of links to the works themselves. It is
   affiliated with the UCLA Graduate School of Education and Information
   Studies (GSE&IS) and the UCLA School of Law.

Child Safety Information

America Links Up, (202) 828-9732, www.americalinksup.org, coordinates a
   public awareness and education campaign sponsored by a broad-based
   coalition of nonprofits, education groups, and corporations concerned
   with providing children with a safe and rewarding experience online.
www.SafeKids.com is operated by the Online Safety Project and is committed
   to the notion that parents, not the government, should regulate their children's online use.

GLOSSARY

Affirm—to uphold a decision reached by a lower court.

Amicus curiae—literally, a "friend of the court," an individual or organization not directly involved in a case who volunteers or is invited by the court to file a brief regarding a point of law or fact directly concerning the lawsuit.

Appeal—to take a case to a higher court for review, to convince the higher court that the lower court's decision was incorrect. The higher court will review only matters that were objected to or argued in the lower court during the trial. No new evidence can be presented on appeal.

Appeals court—an intermediate court of the federal judicial system or a state appellate court. Not all states have intermediate-level courts, but of those that do, many are called the Court of Appeals (or in California and Louisiana, the Court of Appeal). In some states, appeals are divided between a court of criminal appeals and a court of civil appeals.

Brief—a formal written document prepared by an attorney that sets forth the facts and legal arguments in support of a lawsuit. Briefs are filed by either party in a lawsuit (or by an *amicus curiae*).

Burden of proof—the responsibility to produce enough evidence in support of a fact or issue to persuade a judge or jury.

Case—a civil or criminal lawsuit or action; a question contested before a court.

Case law—law established by judicial decisions, as distinguished from law created by legislation.

Certiorari—a writ issued by a superior court—such as the U.S. Supreme Court—at its discretion and at the request of a petitioner, to order a lower court to supply the record of a case to the Court for its review. Parties file a writ of certiorari to have a case from a U.S. Court of Appeals reviewed by the Supreme Court. The Supreme Court may also grant a writ of certiorari to review a decision by a state's highest court when it raises a question about the validity of a federal law, or of a state law on constitutional grounds. Writs of certiorari also are used within state court systems.

Cite—to quote or refer to a precedent or authority.

Civil law—the body of law dealing with the rights of individuals, as opposed to criminal law.

Class action—a lawsuit brought by one person or group on behalf of all persons who have the same interests in the litigation and whose rights or liabilities can be more efficiently determined as a group than in a series of individual suits.

Concurring opinion—an opinion by a judge who agrees with the result reached by the court in a case but not with the reasoning used to reach it.

Constitution—a written document containing the fundamental principles and rules of a nation, state, or social group that determine the powers and duties of the government and guarantee certain rights to the people, and to which all other laws must conform.

Contempt of court (civil and criminal)—Civil contempt is the failure to do something for the benefit of another party after being ordered to do so by a court. Criminal contempt occurs when a person exhibits disrespect for a court or obstructs the administration of justice.

Criminal law—the body of law that deals with the enforcement of laws and the punishment of people who break them.

Defendant—in a civil action, the party denying or defending itself against charges brought by a plaintiff. In a criminal action, the person indicted for breaking the law.

Dismissal—a court order ending a case.

Dissenting opinion—an opinion by a judge who disagrees with the result reached by the court in a case.

Due process—judicial proceedings carried out regularly, fairly, and in accordance with established rules and principles. The Fifth and Fourteenth Amendments to the Constitution contain a "due process clause," which guarantees that Americans may not be deprived of life, liberty, or property by the government until fair and usual procedures have been followed.

Equal protection—a guarantee under the Fourteenth Amendment that a state must treat an individual or a class of individuals (such as women and African Americans) the same as it treats other individuals and classes in similar circumstances. In reviewing claims of denial of equal protection, a court will uphold legislation that has a rational basis unless the law affects a fundamental right or involves a suspect classification, such as race, or otherwise affects a category requiring heightened review. (See *rational basis test, intermediate scrutiny,* or *strict scrutiny.*)

Federal court—a court established by the federal government with jurisdiction over questions of federal law and lawsuits between persons from different states.

Habeas corpus—literally, "have the body"; a writ issued to inquire whether a person is lawfully imprisoned or detained. The writ demands that the persons holding the prisoner justify his detention or release him.

Indictment—a formal written statement of offenses against an individual based on evidence presented by a prosecutor from a grand jury.

Injunction—a court order prohibiting an individual or group from performing a particular act. A defendant who violates an injunction is subject to a penalty for contempt.

Intermediate scrutiny—a level of judicial scrutiny that courts apply to statutes involving the classification of people (such as by sex) to ensure equal protection of the law. Intermediate scrutiny is a tougher standard to meet than the rational basis test but is not as severe as strict scrutiny.

Judgment—the official decision or determination of a court in a case. Also called "decision" and "opinion."

Majority opinion—an opinion in a case written in which a majority of the judges on the court join.

Moot—immaterial or already resolved; abstract or purely academic.

Petitioner—someone who files a petition with a court seeking action or relief, including the plaintiff or appellant. When a writ of certiorari is granted by the Supreme Court, the party seeking review is called the petitioner, and the party responding is called the respondent.

Plaintiff—an individual or group that institutes a legal action or claim.

Plurality opinion—a decision in which a majority of judges on the court agree with the result reached but not with *how* it was reached.

Prosecutor—an individual who institutes and carries on a criminal action.

Rational basis test—a test less intensive than strict scrutiny or intermediate review that involves determining whether a statutory or regulatory classification of persons (i.e., sound reason) has a "rational basis" and does not deny members of the class equal protection under the Constitution.

Remand—to send back. After making a decision in a case, a higher court often remands the case to the court from which it came for further action in light of the higher court's decision.

Respondent—the individual or group compelled to answer or defend claims or questions posed in a court by a petitioner; also, the person or group against whom a petition, such as a writ of *habeas corpus* seeking relief, is brought; or a person or group who wins at trial and defends that outcome on appeal.

Review—a judicial examination and reconsideration of the legality or constitutionality of something, such as a lower court decision or governmental action.

Separation of church and state—the separation of religion and government required under the Establishment Clause of the U.S. Constitution, which forbids the government from establishing a religion or preferring one religion over another, and that protects religious freedom from governmental intrusion.

Separation of powers—the constitutional doctrine that allocates the powers of national government among three branches: the legislative, which is empowered to make laws; the executive, which is required to carry out the laws; and the judicial, whose job it is to interpret and adjudicate (hear and decide) legal disputes.

Standard of proof—the level of certainty and degree of evidence necessary to establish proof in a criminal or civil proceeding.

State court—a court established in accordance with a state constitution and other laws that has the jurisdiction to adjudicate matters of state law.

Statute—a written law enacted by the legislative branch of a state or federal government.

Strict scrutiny—the highest level of scrutiny courts can apply in determining the constitutionality of laws that allegedly violate equal protection of the law. To meet strict scrutiny, a law must satisfy two requirements: (1) it must serve a compelling state interest; and (2) it must be narrowly tailored to serve that interest.

Summary opinion—a legal decision that does not give a case full consideration; an instance in which a court decides a case without having the parties submit briefs on the merits of the case or present oral arguments before the court.

Trial—a judicial examination of issues of fact or law that are disputed by parties for the purpose of determining the rights of the parties.

U.S. Supreme Court—the highest court in the judicial branch of the U.S. government; the court of last resort.

Vacate—to make void, annul, or rescind the decision of a lower court.

Writ—a written order issued in the name of a court telling someone to perform or not perform acts specified in the order.

Sources: Glossary online at www.lawyers.com/lawyers-com/content/glossary/glossary-html; and Victoria Neufeldt, editor in chief, *Webster's New World Dictionary*, 3d ed. (New York: Simon & Schuster, 1988).

NOTES

CLEANSPEAK: A LOOK AT WEB CENSORSHIP

1. Cyber Dialogue, the 1999 Internet Consumer Survey, at www.cyberdialogue.com.

2. *Ibid.*

3. Letter to the editor, *Time*, July 24, 1995, responding to a July 5, 1995, cover story on "Cyberporn."

4. *Ibid.*

5. In 1925, the United States Supreme Court ruled that the protections of the First Amendment's rights of free speech and the press apply through the Fourteenth Amendment to actions by state and local governments as well. See *Gitlow v. New York*, 268 U.S. 652, 666 (1925).

6. The Freedom Forum Online, "First Amendment Timeline," at p. 118.

7. *Ibid.*

8. See "Internet Stuck in Legal Limbo," on page 14 for instances when the Supreme Court has applied less stringent standards.

9. See *ACLU v. Reno II*, 521 U.S. 844, 864–71 (1997).

10. *Id.*

11. *Id.*

12. *Id.*

13. See *Regina v. Hicklin*, L.R.-Q.B. 361 (Eng. 1868).

14. Recognizing that "it is neither realistic nor constitutionally sound to read the First Amendment as requiring that the people of Maine or Mississippi accept public depiction of conduct found tolerable in Las Vegas or New York City," the Court left it up to individual communities to decide what they considered obscene rather than imposing a national standard. 413 U.S. at 33.

15. 413 U.S. at 16. In simpler terms, a trial court applying the three-part obscenity test might ask some version of these four questions:

1. Is the work designed to be sexually arousing?
2. Is it arousing in a way that one's local community would consider unhealthy or immoral?
3. Does the work show acts whose depiction is specifically prohibited by state law?
4. Does the work, when taken as a whole, lack significant literary, artistic, scientific, or social value?

If the answer to all four questions is yes, the material will pass the obscenity test, and it will be constitutional to prosecute someone for distributing it. Mike Godwin, "Virtual Community Standards: BBS Obscenity Case Raises New Legal Issues," in Peter Ludlow, ed., *High Noon on the Electronic Frontier: Conceptual Issues in Cyperspace* (Cambridge, MA: MIT Press, 1996), 269, 271.

16. See *Jacobellis v. Ohio*, 378 U.S.184, 197 (1984) (Stewart, J. concurring).

17. *ACLU v. Reno II*, 521 U.S. 844, 875 (1997) *citing Denver Area Ed. Telecom. Consortium v. FCC*, 518 U.S. 727, 759 (1996).

18. 47 U.S.C. §223(a)(1)(B)(ii).

19. 47 U.S.C. §223(d).

20. 141 Cong. Rec. S8332-S8333 (daily ed. June 14, 1995).

21. *ACLU v. Reno I*, 929 F.Supp. 824 (E.D. Pa. June 11, 1996).

22. Because a case with the same name was filed two years later, the three-judge panel decision is referred to as *ACLU v. Reno I*, the first Supreme Court opinion as *ACLU v. Reno II*, and the COPA challenge as *ACLU v. Reno III* (District Court Opinion) and *ACLU v. Reno IV* (Circuit Court Opinion). See *ACLU v. Reno IV*, 217 F.3d. 162, n. 2 *infra*. at p. 78.

23. 521 U.S. at 883.

24. See *ACLU v. Reno II*, 521 U.S. 844, 864–71 (1997).

25. *Id.*

26. *Id.*

27. See Kelly M. Doherty, "www.obscenity.com: An Analysis of Obscenity and Indecency Regulation on the Internet," 32 *Akron Law Review* 259 (1999).

28. ACLU, "Supreme Court Rules: Cyberspace Will Be Free! ACLU Hails Victory in Internet Censorship Challenge," press release, June 26, 1997.

29. 47 U.S.C. §231 (1998).

30. 217 F.3d 162 (3d Cir. 2000) Petition for Certiorari filed No. 00-1293 (U.S. Sup. Ct. Feb. 12, 2001).

31. "Survey of Internet Access Management in Public Libraries: Summary of Findings," prepared for the American Library Association by the Library Research Center, Graduate School of Library and Information Science, University of Illinois (June 2000), at www.ala.org/alaorg/oif/internetusepoli cies.html, p. 2.

32. *Internet Access in Public Schools & Classrooms: 1994–98*, National Center for Education Statistics, February 1999.

33. Enough Is Enough, "Tips for Parents to Protect Children from Internet Predators," at www.enough.org/safeguards.html.

34. *Ibid.*

35. *Ibid.*

36. *Ibid.*

37. American Library Association Intellectual Freedom Committee, "Statement on Library Use of Filtering Software," July 1, 1997, at www.ala. org/alaorg/oif/filt_stm.html.

38. ACLU, "Censorship in a Box: Why Blocking Software Is Wrong for Public Libraries," at http://www.aclu.org/issues/cyber/box.html.

39. Child Online Protection Act, 47 U.S.C.S. § 231 et. seq. (Dec. 12, 2000).

40. Center for Democracy and Technology, "Re: Filtering Mandates in the Labor, Health and Human Services, and Education Appropriations Bill (H.R. 4577)," August 31, 2000, at http://www.cdt.org/speech/filtering/000831educational.html. Signatories include the American Association of School Administrators, the National Education Association, the National Association of Elementary School Principals, the National PTA, and the National School Boards Association.

41. Joe Salkowski, "Update: McCain Won't Flip Switch on Software Filters," *StarNet Dispatches*, January 22, 1998.

42. See ACLU press release at http://www.aclu.org/news/2000/n121800a.html.

The notes in the following sections are part of the court decisions to which they refer. They were written not by the authors of *Justice Talking* but by the various judges and justices responsible for the court decisions.

AMERICAN CIVIL LIBERTIES UNION ET AL. V. RENO II
521 U.S. 844 (1997)

1. "Congress shall make no law . . . abridging the freedom of speech." U.S. Const., amend. 1.

2. The Court made 410 findings, including 356 paragraphs of the parties' stipulation and 54 findings based on evidence received in open court. See 929 F. Supp. at 830, n.9, 842, n.15.

3. An acronym for the network developed by the Advanced Research Project Agency.

4. *Id.*, at 844 (finding 81).

5. *Id.*, at 831 (finding 3).

9. "Web publishing is simple enough that thousands of individual users and small community organizations are using the Web to publish their own personal 'home pages,' the equivalent of individualized newsletters about the person or organization, which are available to everyone on the Web." *Id.*, at 837 (finding 42).

10. *Id.*, at 838 (finding 46).

11. *Id.*, at 844 (finding 82).

12. *Ibid.* (finding 86).

13. *Ibid.* (finding 85).

14. *Id.*, at 848 (finding 117).

15. *Id.*, at 844–845 (finding 88).

16. *Ibid.*

17. *Id.*, at 845 (finding 89).

18. *Id.*, at 842 (finding 72).

19. *Ibid.* (finding 73).

20. *Id.*, at 845 (finding 90): "An e-mail address provides no authoritative information about the addressee, who may use an e-mail 'alias' or an anonymous remailer. There is also no universal or reliable listing of e-mail addresses and corresponding names or telephone numbers, and any such listing would be or rapidly become incomplete. For these reasons, there is no reliable way in many instances for a sender to know if the e-mail recipient is an adult or a minor. The difficulty of e-mail age verification is compounded for mail exploders such as listservs, which automatically send information to all e-mail addresses on a sender's list. Government expert Dr. Olsen agreed that no current technology could give a speaker assurance that only adults were listed in a particular mail exploder's mailing list."

21. *Ibid.* (finding 93).

22. *Id.*, at 846 (finding 102).

23. *Id.*, at 847 (findings 104–106):

"At least some, if not almost all, non-commercial organizations, such as the ACLU, Stop Prisoner Rape or Critical Path AIDS Project, regard charging listeners to access their speech as contrary to their goals of making their materials available to a wide audience free of charge. . . .

"There is evidence suggesting that adult users, particularly casual Web browsers, would be discouraged from retrieving information that required use of a credit card or password. Andrew Anker testified that HotWired has received many complaints from its members about HotWired's registration system, which requires only that a member supply a name, e-mail address and self-created password. There is concern by commercial content providers that age verification requirements would decrease advertising and revenue because advertisers depend on a demonstration that the sites are widely available and frequently visited."

24. See Exon Amendment No. 1268, 141 Cong. Rec. S8120 (June 9, 1995). See also *id.*, at S8087. This amendment, as revised, became § 502 of the Communications Act of 1996, 110 Stat. 133, 47 U.S.C.A. § § 223(a)-(e) (Supp. 1997). Some Members of the House of Representatives opposed the Exon Amendment because they thought it "possible for our parents now to child-proof the family computer with these products available in the private sector." They also thought the Senate's approach would "involve the Federal Government spending vast sums of money trying to define elusive terms that are going to lead to a flood of legal challenges while our kids are unprotected." These Members offered an amendment intended as a substitute for the Exon Amendment, but instead enacted as an additional section of the Act entitled "Online Family Empowerment." See 110 Stat. 137, 47 U.S.C.A. § 230 (Supp. 1997); 141 Cong. Rec. H8468-H8472. No hearings were held on the provisions that became law. See S. Rep. No. 104-23 (1995), p. 9. After the Senate adopted the Exon amendment, however, its Judiciary Committee did conduct a one-day hearing on "Cyberporn and Children." In his opening statement at that hearing, Senator Leahy observed:

It really struck me in your opening statement when you mentioned, Mr. Chairman, that it is the first ever hearing, and you are absolutely right. And yet we had a major debate on the floor, passed legislation overwhelmingly on a subject involving the Internet, legislation that could dramatically change—some would say even wreak havoc—on the Internet. The Senate went in willy-nilly, passed legislation, and never once had a hearing, never once had a discussion other than an hour or so on the floor. *Cyberporn and Children: The Scope of the Problem, the State of the Technology, and the Need for Congressional Action,* Hearing on S. 892 before the Senate Committee on the Judiciary, 104th Cong., 1st Sess., 7–8 (1995).

25. Although the Government and the dissent break § 223(d)(1) into two separate "patently offensive" and "display" provisions, we follow the convention of both parties below, as well the District Court's order and opinion, in describing § 223(d)(1) as one provision.

26. In full, § 223(e)(5) provides:

(5) It is a defense to a prosecution under subsection (a)(1)(B) or (d) of this section, or under subsection (a)(2) of this section with respect to the use of a facility for an activity under subsection (a)(1)(B) of this section that a person—

(A) has taken, in good faith, reasonable, effective, and appropriate actions under the circumstances to restrict or prevent access by minors to a communication specified in such subsections, which may involve any appropriate measures to restrict minors from such communications, including any method which is feasible under available technology; or

(B) has restricted access to such communication by requiring use of a verified credit card, debit account, adult access code, or adult personal identification number.

27. American Civil Liberties Union; Human Rights Watch; Electronic Privacy Information Center; Electronic Frontier Foundation; Journalism Education Association; Computer Professionals for Social Responsibility; National Writers Union; Clarinet Communications Corp.; Institute for Global Communications; Stop Prisoner Rape; AIDS Education Global Information System; Bibliobytes; Queer Resources Directory; Critical Path AIDS Project, Inc.; Wildcat Press, Inc.; Declan McCullagh d/b/a Justice on Campus; Brock Meeks d/b/a Cyberwire Dispatch; John Troyer d/b/a The Safer Sex Page; Jonathan Wallace d/b/a The Ethical Spectacle; and Planned Parenthood Federation of America, Inc.

28. American Library Association; America Online, Inc.; American Booksellers Association, Inc.; American Booksellers Foundation for Free Expression; American Society of Newspaper Editors; Apple Computer, Inc.; Association of American Publishers, Inc.; Association of Publishers, Editors and Writers; Citizens Internet Empowerment Coalition; Commercial Internet Exchange Association; CompuServe Incorporated; Families Against Internet Censorship; Freedom to Read Foundation, Inc.; Health Sciences Libraries Consortium; Hotwired Ventures LLC; Interactive Digital Software Associa-

tion; Interactive Services Association; Magazine Publishers of America; Microsoft Corporation; The Microsoft Network, LLC; National Press Photographers Association; Netcom Online Communication Services, Inc.; Newspaper Association of America; Opnet, Inc.; Prodigy Services Company; Society of Professional Journalists; Wired Ventures, Ltd.

29. 110 Stat. 142–143, note following 47 U.S.C.A. § 223 (Supp. 1997).

30. See also 929 F. Supp. at 877: "Four related characteristics of Internet communication have a transcendent importance to our shared holding that the CDA is unconstitutional on its face. We explain these characteristics in our Findings of Fact above, and I only rehearse them briefly here. First, the Internet presents very low barriers to entry. Second, these barriers to entry are identical for both speakers and listeners. Third, as a result of these low barriers, astoundingly diverse content is available on the Internet. Fourth, the Internet provides significant access to all who wish to speak in the medium, and even creates a relative parity among speakers." According to Judge Dalzell, these characteristics and the rest of the District Court's findings "lead to the conclusion that Congress may not regulate indecency on the Internet at all." *Ibid.* Because appellees do not press this argument before this Court, we do not consider it. Appellees also do not dispute that the Government generally has a compelling interest in protecting minors from "indecent" and "patently offensive" speech.

31. 390 U.S. at 639. We quoted from *Prince v. Massachusetts,* 321 U.S. 158, 166, 88 L. Ed. 645, 64 S. Ct. 438 (1944): "It is cardinal with us that the custody, care and nurture of the child reside first in the parents, whose primary function and freedom include preparation for obligations the state can neither supply nor hinder."

32. Given the likelihood that many E-mail transmissions from an adult to a minor are conversations between family members, it is therefore incorrect for the dissent to suggest that the provisions of the CDA, even in this narrow area, "are no different from the law we sustained in *Ginsberg.*" *Post* at 8.

33. *Cf. Pacifica Foundation v. FCC,* 181 U.S. App. D.C. 132, 556 F.2d 9, 36 (CADC 1977) (Levanthal, J., dissenting), rev'd, *FCC v. Pacifica Foundation,* 438 U.S. 726, 57 L. Ed. 2d 1073, 98 S. Ct. 3026 (1978). When *Pacifica* was decided, given that radio stations were allowed to operate only pursuant to federal license, and that Congress had enacted legislation prohibiting licensees from broadcasting indecent speech, there was a risk that members of the radio audience might infer some sort of official or societal approval of whatever was

heard over the radio, see 556 F.2d at 37, n.18. No such risk attends messages received through the Internet, which is not supervised by any federal agency.

34. Juris. Statement 3 (citing 929 F. Supp. at 831 (finding 3)).

35. "Indecent" does not benefit from any textual embellishment at all. "Patently offensive" is qualified only to the extent that it involves "sexual or excretory activities or organs" taken "in context" and "measured by contemporary community standards."

36. See *Gozlon-Peretz v. United States*, 498 U.S. 395, 404, 112 L. Ed. 2d 919, 111 S. Ct. 840 (1991) ("Where Congress includes particular language in one section of a statute but omits it in another section of the same Act, it is generally presumed that Congress acts intentionally and purposely in the disparate inclusion and exclusion") (internal quotation marks omitted).

37. The statute does not indicate whether the "patently offensive" and "indecent" determinations should be made with respect to minors or the population as a whole. The Government asserts that the appropriate standard is "what is suitable material for minors." Reply Brief for Appellants 18, n.13 (citing *Ginsberg v. New York*, 390 U.S. 629, 633, 20 L. Ed. 2d 195, 88 S. Ct. 1274 (1968)). But the Conferees expressly rejected amendments that would have imposed such a "harmful to minors" standard. See S. Conf. Rep. No. 104-230, p. 189 (1996) (S. Conf. Rep.), 142 Cong. Rec. H1145, H1165–1166 (Feb. 1, 1996). The Conferees also rejected amendments that would have limited the proscribed materials to those lacking redeeming value. See S. Conf. Rep. at 189, 142 Cong. Rec. H1165–1166 (Feb. 1, 1996).

38. Even though the word "trunk," standing alone, might refer to luggage, a swimming suit, the base of a tree, or the long nose of an animal, its meaning is clear when it is one prong of a three-part description of a species of gray animals.

39. 413 U.S. at 30 (Determinations of "what appeals to the 'prurient interest' or is 'patently offensive' . . . are essentially questions of fact, and our Nation is simply too big and too diverse for this Court to reasonably expect that such standards could be articulated for all 50 States in a single formulation, even assuming the prerequisite consensus exists"). The CDA, which implements the "contemporary community standards" language of *Miller*, thus conflicts with the Conferees' own assertion that the CDA was intended "to establish a uniform national standard of content regulation." S. Conf. Rep. at 191.

40. *Accord, Butler v. Michigan*, 352 U.S. 380, 383, 1 L. Ed. 2d 412, 77 S. Ct.

524 (1957) (ban on sale to adults of books deemed harmful to children unconstitutional); *Sable Communications of Cal., Inc. v. FCC*, 492 U.S. 115, 128, 106 L. Ed. 2d 93, 109 S. Ct. 2829 (1989) (ban on "dial-a-porn" messages unconstitutional); *Bolger v. Youngs Drug Products Corp.*, 463 U.S. 60, 73, 77 L. Ed. 2d 469, 103 S. Ct. 2875 (1983) (ban on mailing of unsolicited advertisement for contraceptives unconstitutional).

41. The lack of legislative attention to the statute at issue in *Sable* suggests another parallel with this case. *Compare* 492 U.S. at 129–130 ("Aside from conclusory statements during the debates by proponents of the bill, as well as similar assertions in hearings on a substantially identical bill the year before, . . . the congressional record presented to us contains no evidence as to *how* effective or ineffective the FCC's most recent regulations were or might prove to be. . . . No Congressman or Senator purported to present a considered judgment with respect to how often or to what extent minors could or would circumvent the rules and have access to dial-a-porn messages") with n.24, *supra*.

42. The Government agrees that these provisions are applicable whenever "a sender transmits a message to more than one recipient, knowing that at least one of the specific persons receiving the message is a minor." Opposition to Motion to Affirm and Reply to Juris. Statement 4-5, n.1.

43. The Government asserts that "there is nothing constitutionally suspect about requiring commercial Web site operators . . . to shoulder the modest burdens associated with their use." Brief for Appellants 35. As a matter of fact, however, there is no evidence that a "modest burden" would be effective.

44. Transmitting obscenity and child pornography, whether via the Internet or other means, is already illegal under federal law for both adults and juveniles. See 18 U.S.C. §§ 1464–1465 (criminalizing obscenity); § 2251 (criminalizing child pornography). In fact, when Congress was considering the CDA, the Government expressed its view that the law was unnecessary because existing laws already authorized its ongoing efforts to prosecute obscenity, child pornography, and child solicitation. See 141 Cong. Rec. S8342 (June 14, 1995) (letter from Kent Markus, Acting Assistant Attorney General, U.S. Department of Justice, to Sen. Leahy).

45. Citing *Church of Lukumi Babalu Aye, Inc. v. Hialeah*, 508 U.S. 520, 124 L. Ed. 2d 472, 113 S. Ct. 2217 (1993), among other cases, appellees offer an additional reason why, in their view, the CDA fails strict scrutiny. Because

so much sexually explicit content originates overseas, they argue, the CDA cannot be "effective." Brief for Appellees American Library Association et al. 33–34. This argument raises difficult issues regarding the intended, as well as the permissible scope of, extraterritorial application of the CDA. We find it unnecessary to address those issues to dispose of this case.

46. For the full text of § 223(e)(5), see n.26, *supra*.

47. Thus, ironically, this defense may significantly protect commercial purveyors of obscene postings while providing little (or no) benefit for transmitters of indecent messages that have significant social or artistic value.

48. 929 F. Supp. at 855–856.

AMERICAN CIVIL LIBERTIES UNION ET AL. V. RENO IV 217 F.3D 162 (3RD CIR. 2000)

2. For ease of reference the various applicable cases will be referred to as follows: *ACLU v. Reno*, 929 F. Supp. 824 (E.D. Pa. 1996), hereinafter *Reno I* (addressing CDA); *ACLU v. Reno*, 521 U.S. 844, 138 L. Ed. 2d 874, 117 S. Ct. 2329 (1997), hereinafter *Reno II* (striking down the CDA as unconstitutional); *ACLU v. Reno*, 31 F. Supp. 2d 473 (E.D. Pa. 1999), hereinafter *Reno III* (case currently on appeal addressing constitutionality of COPA).

4. COPA defines the clause "by means of the World Wide Web" as the "placement of material in a computer server–based file archive so that it is publicly accessible, over the Internet, using hypertext transfer protocol or any successor protocol." 47 U.S.C. § 231(e)(1).

5. COPA defines the clause "commercial purposes" as those individuals or entities that are "engaged in the business of making such communications." 47 U.S.C. § 231(e)(2)(A). In turn, COPA defines a person "engaged in the business" as one who makes a communication, or offers to make a communication, by means of the World Wide Web, that includes any material that is harmful to minors, devotes time, attention, or labor to such activities, as a regular course of such person's trade or business, with the objective of earning a profit as a result of such activities (although it is not necessary that the person make a profit or that the making or offering to make such communications be the person's sole or principal business or source of income). *Id.* § 231(e)(2)(B).

6. In the House Report that accompanied the bill that eventually became COPA, this "harmful to minors" test attempts to conform to the standards identified by the Supreme Court in *Ginsberg v. New York*, 390 U.S. 629, 20 L.

Ed. 2d 195, 88 S. Ct. 1274 (1968), as modified by *Miller v. California*, 413 U.S. 15, 37 L. Ed. 2d 419, 93 S. Ct. 2607 (1973) in identifying "patently offensive" material. See H.R. REP. NO. 105-775, at 13 (1998).

7. Under COPA, a minor is defined as one under age seventeen. See 47 U.S.C. § 231(e)(7).

8. The defense also applies if an individual or entity attempts "in good faith to implement a defense" listed above. See *id.* 47 U.S.C. § 231(c)(2).

9. An individual found to have intentionally violated COPA also faces an additional fine of not more than $50,000 for each day of violation. See 47 U.S.C. § 231(a)(2).

13. Other parties joined the ACLU in asserting the unconstitutionality of COPA. For ease of reference, we will refer to all party-plaintiffs as "ACLU" throughout this opinion.

14. The statute provides:

It is an affirmative defense to prosecution under this section that the defendant, in good faith, has restricted access by minors to material that is harmful to minors—

(A) by requiring use of a credit card, debit account, adult access code, or adult personal identification number,

(B) by accepting a digital certificate that verifies age; or

(C) by any other reasonable measures that are feasible under available technology. See 47 U.S.C. § 231(c).

15. It now seems that those with a valid credit card who wish to acquire an adult PIN may do so without cost using a Web service such as www.freecheck.com.

16. We question, however, the effectiveness of actions taken by a minor's parent to supervise or block harmful material by using filtering software. We are of the view that such actions do not constitute government action, and we do not consider this to be a lesser restrictive means for the government to achieve its compelling interest. See also n.24 *supra*. But see *United States v. Playboy Entertainment Group*, 529 U.S. 803, 120 S. Ct. 1878, 146 L. Ed. 2d 865, 2000 WL 646196 (U.S. 2000).

17. See *Reno III*, 31 F. Supp. 2d at 479.

18. The Supreme Court has recognized that each medium of expression may permit special justifications for regulation. See *Southeastern Promotions, Ltd. v. Conrad*, 420 U.S. 546, 557, 43 L. Ed. 2d 448, 95 S. Ct. 1239 (1975); *Red Lion Broadcasting Co. v. FCC*, 395 U.S. 367, 23 L. Ed. 2d 371, 89 S. Ct. 1794

(1969); *FCC v. Pacifica Foundation*, 438 U.S. 726, 57 L. Ed. 2d 1073, 98 S. Ct. 3026 (1978). For example, broadcast media, due to the history of extensive government regulation, its "invasive" nature, and the scarcity of available frequencies at its inception justified heightened regulation. See, e.g., *Turner Broadcasting System, Inc. v. FCC*, 512 U.S. 622, 637–38, 129 L. Ed. 2d 497, 114 S. Ct. 2445 (1994); *Sable Communications of Cal., Inc. v. FCC*, 492 U.S. 115, 128, 106 L. Ed. 2d 93, 109 S. Ct. 2829 (1989). See also *United States v. Playboy Entertainment Group, Inc.*, 529 U.S. 803, 120 S. Ct. 1878, 146 L. Ed. 2d 865, 2000 WL 646196 (U.S. 2000). However, the Supreme Court has also recognized that these same elements, which justified heightened regulation of the broadcast medium, do not exist in cyberspace. See *ACLU v. Reno*, 521 U.S. 844, 868, 138 L. Ed. 2d 874, 117 S. Ct. 2329 (1997). The Internet has not been historically subject to regulation. Nor has the Internet suffered from a scarcity of available frequencies. See *id.* at 869–70. Therefore, the Supreme Court held that there is "no basis for qualifying the level of First Amendment scrutiny that should be applied to this [cyberspace] medium." *Id.* at 870.

19. As a result, we do not find it necessary to address the District Court's analysis of the definition of "commercial purposes"; whether the breadth of the forms of content covered by COPA could have been more narrowly tailored; whether the affirmative defenses impose too great a burden on Web publishers or whether those affirmative defenses should have been included as elements of the crime itself; whether COPA's inclusion of criminal as well as civil penalties was excessive; whether COPA is designed to include communications made in chat rooms, discussion groups and links to other Web sites; whether the government is entitled to so restrict communications when children will continue to be able to access foreign Web sites and other sources of material that is harmful to them; what taken "as a whole" should mean in the context of the Web and the Internet; or whether the statute's failure to distinguish between material that is harmful to a six year old versus a sixteen year old is problematic.

We recognize that in focusing on the "contemporary community standards" aspect of COPA we are affirming the District Court's ruling on a ground other than that emphasized by the District Court. See *Paac v. Rizzo*, 502 F.2d 306, 308 n.1 (1974).

20. The Sable court found that: "Sable is free to tailor its messages, on a selective basis, if it so chooses, to the communities it chooses to serve. While Sable may be forced to incur some costs in developing and implementing a

system for screening the locale of incoming calls, there is no constitutional impediment to enacting a law that may impose such costs on a medium electing to provide these messages." *Sable* 492 U.S. at 125–26.

21. Even if we were to overlook the unconstitutional overbreadth of the COPA "contemporary community standards" test and if COPA were to be deemed effective, it still would not eliminate much of the harmful material which a minor could access. For example, minors could still access harmful material published by non-commercial Web publishers, and by foreign Web publishers. Thus, for example, materials "harmful to minors" but generated in foreign communities with contemporary community standards far more liberal than those of any state in the United States may, nevertheless, remain available and be exposed to children in the United States by means of the Web/Internet, despite COPA's restrictions.

22. Although our concern here has been with the overbreadth of the "contemporary community standards" clause, we recognize that if we were to address that portion of COPA which speaks to communications made for commercial purposes, 47 U.S.C. § 231(e)(2)(A), the Supreme Court has taught that "for the purposes of applying the overbreadth doctrine . . . it remains relevant to distinguish between commercial and noncommercial speech." *Village of Schaumburg v. Citizens for a Better Environment*, 444 U.S. 620, 632 n.7, 63 L. Ed. 2d 73, 100 S. Ct. 826 (1980). For instance, it has declined to apply the overbreadth doctrine to statutes regulating commercial advertising:

> The justification for the application of overbreadth analysis applies weakly, if at all, in the ordinary commercial context. . . . There are "commonsense differences" between commercial speech and other varieties. Since advertising is linked to commercial well-being, it seems unlikely that such speech is particularly susceptible to being crushed by overbroad regulation. Moreover, concerns for uncertainty in determining the scope of protection are reduced.

Bates v. State Bar of Arizona, 433 U.S. 350, 380–81, 53 L. Ed. 2d 810, 97 S. Ct. 2691 (1977) (citations omitted). See also *Central Hudson Gas & Elec. Corp. v. Public Serv. Comm'n of New York*, 447 U.S. 557, 564 n.6, 65 L. Ed. 2d 341, 100 S. Ct. 2343 (1980) ("Commercial speech, the offspring of economic self-interest, is a hardy breed of expression that is not 'particularly susceptible to being crushed by overbroad regulation.' ").

However, although COPA regulates the commercial content of the Web, it amounts to neither a restriction on commercial advertising nor a regulation of activity occurring "in the ordinary commercial context." *Bates*, 433 U.S. at 380–81. As we have noted, the Web is a new type of medium which allows the average person with relatively little capital investment to place content on it for a commercial purpose. The speech such Web sites provide is in far greater danger of being stifled by government regulation than the commercial advertising at issue in cases such as Bates and Central Hudson Gas.

As the Supreme Court has also made clear, the benefits gained by the challenged statute must also outweigh the burden imposed on commercial speech. See *Elrod v. Burns*, 427 U.S. 347, 363, 49 L. Ed. 2d 547, 96 S. Ct. 2673 (1976); *Greater New Orleans Broad. Ass'n, Inc. v. United States*, 527 U.S. 173, 188, 144 L. Ed. 2d 161, 119 S. Ct. 1923 (1999) (in regulating commercial speech, "the regulation may not be sustained if it provides only ineffective or remote support for the government's purpose."). The Supreme Court has repeatedly stated that the free speech rights of adults may not be reduced to allow them to read only what is acceptable for children. See *Bolger v. Youngs Drug Prods. Corp.*, 463 U.S. 60, 74-75, 77 L. Ed. 2d 469, 103 S. Ct. 2875 (1983) ("The level of discourse reaching a mailbox simply cannot be limited to that which would be suitable for a sandbox."). See also *Sable*, 492 U.S. at 127. Therefore, there is no inconsistency between our position that COPA is overbroad, and the line of authority refusing to apply overbreadth analysis to certain types of commercial speech.

23. These costs with respect to Web publishers and to those who desire access to those Web sites were enumerated by the District Court in its findings of fact.

24. Although much attention at the District Court level was focused on the availability, virtues and effectiveness of voluntary blocking or filtering software that can enable parents to limit the harmful material to which their children may otherwise be exposed, the parental hand should not be looked to as a substitute for a congressional mandate. See also n.16 *supra*.

25. "When sensitive matters of freedom of speech collide with images of children's vulnerability, and are framed in terms of the battle between good and evil, even well intentioned people can lose sight of fundamental constitutional principles." Catherine J. Ross, *Anything Goes: Examining the State's Interest in Protecting Children from Controversial Speech*, 53 Vand. L. Rev. 427, 521 (2000).

MAINSTREAM LOUDOUN ET AL., PLAINTIFFS, V. BOARD OF TRUSTEES OF THE LOUDOUN COUNTY LIBRARY ET AL., DEFENDANTS
2 F. SUPP. 2d 783 (E.D. VA. 1998)

1. In a February 24, 1998, Order, this Court granted a Motion to Intervene as Plaintiffs made by several individuals and organizations which publish speech on the Internet. Intervenors argue that defendants have unconstitutionally interfered with their First Amendment rights as speakers to communicate with Loudoun County library patrons. The intervenors' claim is not explicitly at issue in the motions now before the Court.

4. For purposes of defendants' Motion to Dismiss for Failure to State a Claim or, in the Alternative, for Summary Judgment, the Court accepts plaintiffs' description of the unblocking policy as accurate. See Complaint PP127–29.